GENERATION TO GENERATION

Realizing the Promise of Family Literacy

BY
JACK A. BRIZIUS
AND
SUSAN A. FOSTER

SPONSORED BY THE
NATIONAL CENTER
FOR FAMILY LITERACY

HIGH/SCOPE PRESS
YPSILANTI, MICHIGAN

Published by
HIGH/SCOPE® PRESS

A division of High/Scope® Educational Research Foundation
600 North River Street
Ypsilanti, MI 48198-2898
(313) 485-2000, FAX (313) 485-0704

Design and production: Margaret FitzGerald

Library of Congress Cataloging-in-Publication Data

Brizius, Jack A.
    Generation to generation : realizing the promise of family
literacy / by Jack A. Brizius and Susan A. Foster ; sponsored by the
National Center for Family Literacy.
        p. cm.
    Includes bibliographical references (p.) .
    ISBN 0-929816-54-4 : $19.95
    1. Family literacy programs—United States. I. Foster, Susan A. ,
1948- . II. Title.
LC151.B76 1993   93-10051
302. 2'244—dc20   CIP

Printed in the United States of America

CONTENTS

ACKNOWLEDGMENTS xi

PREFACE xiii

INTRODUCTION xvii

1. FAMILY LITERACY: THE NEED AND THE PROMISE 3

The Need 3

The Promise of Family Literacy 6

Strengthening Families 7

Reforming Our Schools 8

Breaking the Cycle of Poverty and Dependency 11

Why Family Literacy? 11

2. DEFINING FAMILY LITERACY 13

Components of Family Literacy 14

Family Literacy Programs Provide Developmental Experiences
for Young Children 15

Family Literacy Programs Provide Basic Skills Instruction to the
Children's Parents or Primary Caregivers 18

Family Literacy Programs Work With Parents and Children
Together, Helping Them to Share in the Learning Experience 19

Family Literacy Programs Bring Parents Together in Peer Support
Groups to Share Experiences and Overcome Obstacles to Family
Learning 19

Why Worry About Definitions? 21

Related Intergenerational Approaches 22

3. THE HISTORY OF FAMILY LITERACY 25

The Roots of Family Literacy 25

Family Literacy and Public Policy: Kentucky's Pace Program 27

The Kenan Project **29**

The National Center for Family Literacy **31**

Even Start **34**

The Barbara Bush Foundation for Family Literacy **39**

The Bureau of Indian Affairs Initiative **42**

The Apple Partnership and Family Literacy **43**

Head Start and Family Literacy **45**

State Initiatives **48**

Summary: Significant Change in Less Than a Decade 50

4. THE RESEARCH: HOW DO WE KNOW IF FAMILY LITERACY WORKS? 53

Dividing Up the Research Questions 54

Early Childhood Development **55**

Adult Literacy **59**

Adults Can Make Significant Improvements in Their Literacy Skills **59**

Adults Appear to Learn in Different Ways Than Children **60**

Adults Who Are Learning English as a Second Language Have a Different Challenge From Most Low-Literate Adults **61**

Adults Must Be Strongly Motivated to Make a Sustained Effort to Increase Literacy **61**

Programs That Provide a Support System for Adults Appear to Have Better Results Than Those That Do Not **61**

Time Together **62**

Peer Support **63**

Putting Together the Elements of Family Literacy 63

Early Results From Family Literacy Evaluations **65**

Family Literacy Programs Serve People With Significant Economic, Social, and Educational Problems **68**

Family Literacy Programs Help Families With Many Problems Related to Lack of Education and Poverty **69**

In Family Literacy Programs Providing All Four Program Components, Children Are Gaining Real Benefits **70**

Parents Are Participating in and Supporting Their Children's Education **71**

Research for the Future of Family Literacy 72

5. BUILDING A COMMUNITY FAMILY LITERACY PROGRAM 75

Five Steps for Family Literacy in Your Community 76

Prepare Your Community for Family Literacy **76**

Get a Collaborative Group Together **77**

Define Your Community and the People You Plan to Serve **78**

Estimate How Many People Can Benefit From the Program **78**

Assess the Community's Human Resources **80**

Examine the Possibilities for Funding **81**

Tailor a Program to Suit Your Community's Needs **82**

The Group-Based Model **82**

The Home-Based Model **91**

The Combination Model **92**

Workplace-Based Model **93**

Obtain Institutional Support **94**

Raise the Resources for Excellence **95**

Implement and Evaluate Your Program **98**

6. DEVELOPING A STATE FAMILY LITERACY INITIATIVE 103

Political Leaders: How Do They Feel About Family Literacy? 103

Building the Constituency for Family Literacy 105

Find Some Allies **105**

Portray Family Literacy in the Context of Key State Priorities **106**

Make Sure That Adult Literacy Efforts Include Family Literacy **107**

Develop the Efficiency Argument **107**

Finding Champions 108

Putting Together a Family Literacy Package 109

Who? **109**

What? **110**

When? **112**

Where? **112**

How? **113**

Building in Evaluation From the Start 114

State Initiatives: A Few Victories So Far 115

Hawaii **115**

North Carolina **117**

Louisiana **119**

Illinois **120**

Why We Need State Leadership 121

7. CHALLENGE FOR THE FAMILY LITERACY MOVEMENT 123

The Nation Needs a Family Literacy Movement 124

Arriving at a National Definition of Family Literacy **124**

Clarifying Service Delivery Models **126**

Defining the Relationship of Family Literacy Programs to Other Social and Educational Programs **126**

State and Federal Governments Need to Support Family Literacy in a Coherent Way 127

Clarifying Family Literacy's Public Policy Niche **127**

Clarifying the Role of State and Federal Governments in Family Literacy **128**

Family Literacy Programs Must Be Accountable 128

Documenting Our Successes; Learning From Our Failures **128**

Improving Assessment and Evaluation **129**

We Must Build an Infrastructure to Support the Family Literacy Movement 130

Creating an Institutional Infrastructure **130**

Providing Increased Training and Training Across Programs **130**

The Research Agenda 131

Determining the Outcomes of Family Literacy Programs **132**

Reflecting the Differences in History and Culture of the Community in Which Family Literacy Programs Are Operating **133**

Expanding the Concept of the Family in Family Literacy **133**

Fitting Family Literacy Into a Model of Lifelong Learning and Work-Force Education **133**

Searching for the Relationship Between Taught and Acquired Literacy in Family Literacy Programs **134**

Finding Family Literacy's Relationship to Community Change **134**

Finding Out How Parents, Teachers, and Students Change Attitudes and Behaviors Through Family Literacy **135**

The Practice Agenda 136

Promoting Experimentation and Innovation **136**

Increasing the Sensitivity of Family Literacy Programs to the Goals of Participants **136**

Assuring That Programs Focus on Quality Outcomes and Their Relationship to Individual Goals **137**

Relating Family Literacy to Other Reforms **137**

Developing Family Literacy Models That Include Cross-Cultural Groupings **138**

Using Existing Networks for Furthering Goals of
Family Literacy **138**

Linking Family Literacy Programs to Lifelong Learning **138**

The Policy Agenda 138

Defining the Costs and Benefits of Family Literacy Programs **139**

Moving From a Deficit Model of Family Literacy to an
Assets-Based Model **139**

Encouraging More Local Policy Development and Debate **140**

Educating Policymakers and the Public About
Family Literacy **140**

Defining the State Role in Providing Support for
Family Literacy **140**

Enhancing the Federal Role in Family Literacy **141**

Building More Cohesion Among Federal and State Policies **141**

8. THE FUTURE OF FAMILY LITERACY 143

The Family Literacy Movement 143

Growth at the Grassroots Level 144

Where Should We Go From Here? 146

Providing Family Literacy Nationwide **147**

Building a National Infrastructure **148**

Continuous Quality Improvement in Family Literacy **149**

What Each of Us Can Do to Help 150

BIBLIOGRAPHY 153

ACKNOWLEDGMENTS

We gratefully acknowledge the John D. and Catherine T. MacArthur Foundation for their support of research and development toward high-quality literacy programs and, particularly, their encouragement of family literacy. We are especially appreciative of their underwriting for this manuscript.

This book could not have been written without the support of numerous people and organizations who believe in the power and the promise of family literacy.

The William R. Kenan, Jr. Charitable Trust has provided the means for family literacy to spread throughout the country by its support of and encouragement to the National Center for Family Literacy.

Our special thanks to the following members of the National Planning Committee of the 1992 National Conference on Family Literacy who contributed valuable advice in planning and reviewing the book's contents: Bobby Anderson, North Carolina Department of Community Colleges; Sue Berg, Hawaii Office of Children and Youth; Vivian Gadsden, National Center on Adult Literacy; Peter Gerber, the John D. and Catherine T. MacArthur Foundation; Mary Jean LeTendre, United States Department of Education; Don Snodgrass, North Carolina Department of Community Colleges; Benita Somerfield, the Barbara Bush Foundation for Family Literacy; David Weikart, High/Scope Educational Research Foundation; and Heather Weiss, Harvard Family Research Project.

The following staff members of the National Center for Family Literacy have shared their experiences and knowledge and provided guidance for this publication: Connie Brown, Mary Anne Cronan, Bonnie Freeman, Rebecca King, Robert Mueller, Susan Paull, Meta Potts, Robert Spillman, and Nancy Spradling.

PREFACE

This volume depicts the realization of a vision, a vision shared by many across the country — those who saw the problems of undereducated adults, the tragedy of at-risk children, the cycle of undereducation, disadvantage, and despair, and found the sight intolerable. They felt strongly that we as a society must set our sights instead on possibilities — on a better future for America's at-risk families.

This new vision came to be called family literacy, and for those of us who have watched the movement grow, watched the vision develop from a gleam in our collective eyes, it is particularly gratifying to see in this book documentation of what we have accomplished. We can see the efforts of all the families, teachers, administrators, policymakers, founders, friends, and supporters in programs across the nation.

To witness the progress this book describes and to understand what the family literacy movement has meant for thousands of parents and children is to experience one of those rare and rewarding moments when we feel the joy of real accomplishment. And so, although we know there is a long way to go and many parents and children still to reach, I think it is appropriate to take advantage of the occasion of the publication of this book to extend congratulations and appreciation.

It is surely appropriate to applaud the courage we see daily in family literacy programs. It takes courage for parents to come back to school, look "old ghosts" in the face, put mistakes in the past, and dare to dream again. And it takes courage for parents to keep on trying in spite of the barriers and frustrations they face as they work for a better future for themselves and their families.

The parents' courage is matched by their teachers' spirit. What does it take to change your focus, your teaching approach, your very way of thinking, in order to become a team member in this new program? What a challenge it becomes to leave behind the familiar status of "early childhood teacher" or "adult educator" for a new role as "family literacy instructor." It takes courage to accept the expanded focus of this new vision and to find a way to deal with the other than educational needs of families.

And what about those who first decided this idea was worth the risk—the trustees of the William R. Kenan, Jr. Charitable Trust who had the courage to move from their traditional funding pattern to support programs serving the most basic needs of families, and the executives of the Toyota Motor Corporation who were bold enough to make a corporate commitment that has helped to introduce this innovation to America's cities? We remember, too, the school principals, legislators, community leaders, and political figures at all levels of government who have put their time, money, and influence behind the movement. It takes courage to try something new, something that challenges disciplinary divisions and bureaucratic structures, something that requires new collaborations within programs, across agencies, and throughout communities. This book tells a tale of vision, initiative, and courage.

But it also speaks of teamwork. Teamwork is a major theme in family literacy. Families work as teams in pursuit of learning — for the good of individuals and the family as a whole. Teaching teams create a uniquely integrated learning environment for children and parents. Schools, community agencies, and organizations collaborate with government and the private sector to provide funding and other supports for families and programs. I applaud the efforts of all these people whose work gave us a story to tell.

I appreciate also those who had a part in telling the story, who accepted the challenge of defining the family literacy movement, detailing the lessons we have learned, and suggesting directions for the future. To all these old friends and colleagues, and any "new recruits," I say congratulations and good luck. I hope you are encouraged by what you read on these pages and inspired to join in as we take the next steps in family literacy.

We must now take to heart the lessons of the past and continue to follow the vision, so we can develop an infrastructure for our programs across the nation and ensure that quality services for America's most in-need families will continue. It has been a privilege to be a part of family literacy's brief but exciting history. Let us move on from here with our sights on the future.

SHARON DARLING, PRESIDENT
National Center for Family Literacy

INTRODUCTION

When Rhonda, a young mother in Appalachian Kentucky, gets off the school bus on a foggy morning, and holding daughter Jennifer's hand, walks into the school, she is not thinking about family literacy or its future. When Walter, a single father, settles in front of a computer screen in a rural North Carolina schoolhouse to practice his reading, he is not concerned with the future of the family literacy movement. When Louise, a three-year-old toddler from Los Angeles, plays with her blocks at a preschool on the south side, she is not aware of her part in a new national movement.

When President Geroge Bush and the nation's governors met in 1989 and established six goals for national education reform, they were not deliberating the future of family literacy. As the Hawaii legislature debated a sweeping new law establishing a family literacy demonstration, they were only briefly aware of their role as leaders in strengthening families. When Congress passed a $70 million appropriation for Even Start, a federal family literacy program, most members barely noticed that they had validated and strengthened a growing national movement.

Yet in actions such as these, all these people and thousands more like them have become a vanguard, transforming a deceptively simple and appealing idea into a national movement. In less than a decade, the simple idea that parents and children could learn together for the betterment of both has taken root and flourished all across America. Today, family literacy is a movement with momentum, an idea whose time has come.

Family literacy started as a seed of an idea, took root in a few programs in a few places, spread like wildflowers across a prairie, and now is established as a key feature in America's public policy landscape. It spread because family literacy provides a way of cutting through two generations of poverty and ignorance with one simple approach. It spread because its timing was impeccable and because it works.

This book is about family literacy and its future.

It traces the history of family literacy as an idea, as fledgling programs, and as a public policy movement. It tackles some tough definitional issues surrounding a seemingly simple and appealing idea. This book also shows state policymakers and program managers how to anticipate and grapple with the issues surrounding family literacy. Then it suggests how you can start new family literacy programs tailored to your own communities. Finally, it addresses key issues about the future of the family literacy concept and the movement that has grown up around it.

If you are already part of the family literacy movement, you have probably experienced the satisfaction of seeing a family achieve things they never thought were possible. You are contributing to an all-important national effort to break the cycle of poverty and dependency. You are part of a growing movement of people working to realize a simple ideal: *that parents and children can learn together, and in learning together can overcome the most difficult odds.*

If you have not yet joined this movement, we hope this book will act as your guide to family literacy and its future. We explain what family literacy is, where it came from, and how it works. We hope to enlist you in the movement, show you how to start a family literacy program in your own community, and how to become involved at the state and national levels. Most important, we want to start you working toward a new vision of family literacy that breaks the intergenerational bonds of poverty and ignorance in your community and state.

GENERATION TO GENERATION

Realizing the Promise of Family Literacy

Chapter 1

FAMILY LITERACY: THE NEED AND THE PROMISE

Family literacy is an approach to solving the problems of intergenerational poverty and undereducation that responds to a burning need with a promise. The need is to make practical progress in breaking the cycle of poverty. The promise is to educate parents and children together so that they can lift themselves out of poverty and fulfill their dreams.

THE NEED

Some people think that there is little we can do to reduce poverty and prevent dependency. For several decades, we have heard the litany of facts reminding us of the persistence of poverty and ignorance in America. As the economy has grown slowly over the past two decades, we have not made much progress in ending the scourge of poverty and dependency. As the twentieth century draws to a close, the indicators of America's social and economic health are troubling:

- One of six babies born in America today is to a teenage mother.

3

Forty percent of these teen mothers have an eighth grade education or less. Fewer than half will complete high school.

• One-fifth of our nation's first graders are living in poverty. About half of all poor children begin school as much as two years behind their peers in preschool skills.

• About one-third of our young people do not complete high school on their first try. Poor children are three to four times more likely than other children to drop out of school. Many of those who do complete school read, write, and compute at a sixth-grade level.

• Tens of millions of American adults are unable to apply basic reading, writing, and math skills in adult life con-

The promise of family literacy is to educate parents and children together so that they can lift themselves out of poverty and fulfill their dreams.

texts. Millions more are only marginally literate. One in five American workers reads at an eighth-grade level or below.

- At the same time, our economy requires more skilled, productive workers and citizens. By the year 2000, virtually all the jobs worth having will require a high school education, and most high-wage jobs will require post-secondary training. Eighty-five percent of the work force in the year 2000 has already left school.[1]

The problems facing our families are mounting, passed down from generation to generation. Living in undereducated families, children of the poor often fail to achieve a solid grounding in basic skills. Their schools may offer remediation, but these services come too late for children from unstable homes and violent neighborhoods. The home provides neither literacy nor support for learning. Too often, educational attainment is discouraged by families and friends. Cut off from the mainstream, many young people drop out of school as early as possible.

Since the fathers of many of these children are undereducated and cannot find jobs, teen mothers often turn to public assistance for survival. Trapped in the same environment that limited their own achievements, many of these women never manage to pull themselves out of poverty. Their self-esteem becomes as low as their educational attainment, and these attitudes are communicated daily to their children. They begin their lives much as their parents and grandparents did, behind from the start and never quite able to catch up.

For those children who do live with both father and mother, if the parents are undereducated and hold low-skill jobs, the expectations and educational achievement of the children are too often stunted by the lack of literacy in the household. Undereducated parents, fatigued and discouraged by dead-end jobs, may not have the time, skills, awareness, and confidence to assist their children in learning. And so the cycle repeats itself, with young people emerging from their educational experiences ill prepared for productive work, ill prepared for responsible citizenship.

In the face of what sometimes appears to be an overwhelming set of staggeringly complex problems, we may be tempted to view possible

Parents and children can learn together and enhance the lives of each.

solutions with skepticism. Most of us, however, have faith that there are solutions to be found, to some — if not all — of the problems of poverty and dependency. New and more effective approaches to breaking the cycle of poverty and dependency need to be discovered and developed.

Poverty, ignorance, and despair can be carried down from generation to generation, or we can intervene and refuse to allow this vicious cycle to continue. In a search for ways to intervene with dignity and success, we have developed family literacy. Family literacy is an approach that can help break the cycle of poverty and dependency among families that need a second chance. Family literacy can be a tool available to every community to help break the intergenerational cycle of poverty, undereducation, and dependency.

THE PROMISE OF FAMILY LITERACY

Family literacy is based upon a simple but powerful premise: parents and children can learn together and enhance the lives of each other. When parents and children learn together, an appreciation and respect for education is provided for the children, which paves the way for school success; parents acquire new skills for work and home and a new appreciation of their role as first teacher.

Family literacy helps develop in children and parents alike an appreciation for the value of lifelong learning. Economic realities will require each of us to adapt to a rapidly changing workplace in the next century. To become productive members of the twenty-first-century work force, parents and students must learn how to get, understand, and manipulate information, to prepare for jobs that have not yet been created.

Family literacy has roots in and supports several movements in America: efforts to strengthen the family and provide early childhood education, school reform, and economic development through adult literacy. The family literacy movement has found broad support because it is a way to address our critical national needs to support the family, improve the skills of children and adults, and strengthen our economy.

STRENGTHENING FAMILIES

Family literacy helps strengthen the family because it brings parents and children together as they learn. Parents are taught not only skills such as reading, writing, and math, but also ways of relating to their children more positively and supportively. Family literacy also brings parents together to support each other. Many parents live in an environment that is often difficult and hostile to their success as learners or parents. The support of others who are in similar circumstances and are working toward the same goals can make an important difference.

Family literacy is also based on the knowledge that *most* of what children learn is learned in family settings. Small children soak up not only skills and behavior patterns but attitudes as well. "Parents are the first and most important teachers of their children, and their attitudes convey a critical message about schooling, the work and joy of learning, and the connection between education and the quality of life."[2] As a result, the educational background of parents has a direct— sometimes positive and sometimes devastating — effect on the prospects of children when they enter school.

Family literacy programs strengthen families by providing better models of parent-child interaction, by providing support in changing patterns of family interaction, and by providing children with role models of adults who are placing a high value on upgrading their education — role models that will make a significant difference in children's attitudes toward education.

Family literacy programs not only work with intact, nuclear families, but also help many other kinds of families, from single mothers and their children to grandparents or older siblings who have the primary care-giving responsibilities for young children. Family literacy programs help strengthen all kinds of families.

In an age in which there is much talk about the importance of the family, but more pressure on all kinds of families, family literacy programs are designed to bring families together, to help them learn new skills, including skills in making a family work. Family literacy can be seen within the context of a broad range of efforts to support and strengthen the American family.

REFORMING OUR SCHOOLS

Family literacy programs also contribute to meeting our national goals to improve education throughout America. Even as family literacy recognizes the primacy of the family as educator, it seeks to reach into the schools and change them, to reach a new accommodation among parents, children, and schools. Family literacy programs can provide the essential partnership among schools, parents, and young children to help prepare all parties for a more successful educational experience.

The family literacy movement has grown out of a recognition that we need to restructure and transform our schools — to make them more responsive to the needs of children and adult learners. We must redesign schools to be more responsive to families and communities and better equipped to meet the changing needs of our economy and society.

School reform must be based on what we know about how children learn and about how their home environments prepare them for and support them in learning. We know that in order for children to thrive and learn they must be healthy, well-fed, and rested. They must feel safe and secure. We also recognize these facts:

- The better prepared children are for school, the better they will perform when they get to school. Early language learning is a family affair; children who are read to become better readers.

- Parental involvement in preparing young children for school is absolutely crucial. Although programs offering positive early childhood experiences are effective, the family is still the crucible where most early skills and attitudes emerge.

- Parents who themselves have had negative experiences with school are often reluctant to participate in educational decisions with their children. Just as the pattern of learning is established early among children, whether or not parents will take an active interest in a child's education is determined long before the child enters school.

- Attitudes about learning are as important to success as is the educational program. Positive parental and student attitudes need to be reinforced if they exist. Parents need to be reintroduced to learning in a positive way.

- The higher the parent's educational level and the higher the income of the family, the better chance children have to succeed. If parents' skills are improved and they learn to value education, their incomes will increase, even as they communicate the benefits of education to their children. Families will then be able to afford to support educational efforts of their children more fully.

Many family literacy programs bring together parents, children, and the schools to provide benefits for each that, when added together, equal more than just the parts. Family literacy, for example, teaches parents and children how to support each other in learning. In many programs, parents volunteer to work in the schools long after their children have entered elementary school. In fact, family literacy programs have brought greater parental involvement in schooling wherever they have been implemented.

Family literacy supports education reform by addressing two of the six national educational goals, enunciated by President George Bush and the nation's governors in September 1989. Goal 1 addresses the need for children to be better prepared for school, while Goal 5 aims to improve the literacy of adults. Family literacy supports early childhood development even as it attends to improving the literacy skills of parents. Family literacy can be viewed as an integral part of education reform.

We need family literacy programs to help strengthen our efforts to reform our schools. Our economic future is closely tied to our success in education reform. Education reform will only be successful if schools recognize that the learning environment in the home is just as important as in the school building itself. For many families and children, family literacy can bridge the gap between home and school, enhancing parents' motivation and skills in helping their children learn.

EARNINGS: MONTHLY MEAN

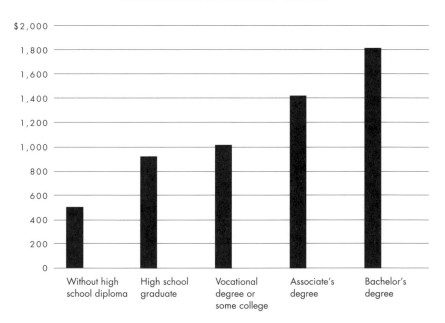

Source: Bureau of the Census–Statistical Brief, February 1991

BREAKING THE CYCLE OF POVERTY AND DEPENDENCY

Family literacy can help break the intergenerational cycle of poverty and dependency. Family literacy improves the educational opportunities for children and parents by providing both learning experiences and group support. In the process, family literacy provides parents with skills that will improve their incomes. It provides disadvantaged children with educational opportunities that can enable them to lift themselves out of poverty and dependency.

Family literacy does not claim to solve all problems of poverty and dependency. It does, however, provide a powerful tool for helping some parents start on the road to economic independence. Family literacy also provides an underpinning of support, encouragement, and educational opportunities for their children.

Family literacy programs help those who need help the most, usually poor and always undereducated parents and children. As such, family literacy is a well-targeted approach to the problems of intergenerational poverty and dependency. Family literacy programs also serve those who are motivated to help themselves, making it more likely that the help offered by family literacy providers will be well used.

WHY FAMILY LITERACY?

In subsequent chapters of this book, we will learn more about family literacy — how it is defined, its history, how to start family literacy programs, and the challenge for the family literacy movement. But before we proceed, we may ask ourselves once again, "Why family literacy?"

The answer is that family literacy proposes a comprehensive strategy to get at the root of school failure and undereducation. Our schools require it. Our economy demands it. Our low-skilled adults need it. Our children deserve nothing less.

ENDNOTES

[1] Sharon Darling, *Family Literacy: The Need and the Promise* (Louisville, KY: The National Center for Family Literacy, 1992), 2–3.

[2] Ibid., 4.

Chapter 2

DEFINING
FAMILY LITERACY

"Family literacy" means different things to different people. For most people, family literacy implies literacy instruction for both parents and children. To some, teaching a mother to read a bedtime story to a child is "family literacy," while to others, family literacy may be home-based instruction for parents in reading to their children. Others classify programs involving parents in developmental child care as "family literacy" efforts. While many of these programs are related to family literacy, not all can be considered family literacy programs. Rather, family literacy programs must be considered as part of a larger family of approaches to breaking the bonds of intergenerational poverty through education and parental support.[1]

Family literacy should be viewed as one line of an extended family of approaches to intergenerational poverty prevention, family support, and education improvement. Other approaches, such as parent-as-first-teacher programs, share certain characteristics with family literacy programs but are separate.

They have their own lineages, histories, and fundamental assumptions. In a sense, programs such as family reading, Parent as Teachers, Mother-Read,® and Home Instruction for Preschool Youth (HIPPY) are all part of an extended clan or kin group of programs of which family literacy is a specific family, with a special ancestry. Like the Smith or Jones families in any community, family literacy programs have special historical lineages, belief systems, and characteristics that distinguish family literacy from other intergenerational education programs.

The reason that we focus on these distinctions is to give context to family literacy, to place it within a group of kindred programs and approaches to intergenerational literacy enhancement and dependency reduction. Family literacy is an important approach, one that has found a great deal of success. But it is only one of a number of valid and similar approaches to the problems of poor families that should complement family literacy in the arsenal of tools available to communities. As such, however, family literacy can be defined specifically, because family literacy programs all share four specific components or characteristics.

COMPONENTS OF FAMILY LITERACY

Each of the major family literacy initiatives in the United States share common definitions of program components. The Barbara Bush Foundation for Family Literacy, for example, describes family literacy programs as characterized by

- Literacy and parenting education for adults

- Prereading and other literacy activities for children

- Time for parents to use their newly acquired skills *with* their children

The federal Even Start program defines very similar components and adds that children should be seven or younger to qualify.

The most extensive definition of program components for family literacy is provided by the National Center for Family Literacy. According to the Center, family literacy programs have the following four characteristics, each of which is an important component in the definition of family literacy:

- Family literacy programs provide developmental experiences for young children.
- Family literacy programs provide basic skills instruction to the children's parents or primary caregivers.
- Family literacy programs work with parents and children together, helping them to share in the learning experience.
- Family literacy programs bring parents together in peer support groups to share experiences and overcome obstacles to family learning.

These four elements must work together, but it is not crucial where they are working, in what order, or at what time of the day or week. The time or setting is not the critical feature that distinguishes family literacy; the four program elements, together with enough time and intensity of activity, define successful family literacy programs. (See "Family Literacy Programs: Four Examples" sidebar on p. 16.) Family literacy programs operate nearly anywhere, day or night. In fact, some of the most successful family literacy programs do not operate with rigid timetables, but are built around the needs and schedules of the participants. Although most family literacy programs have been school- or community-based, an increasing number are workplace-based. Home-based and nighttime programs are also proliferating, as family literacy responds to the needs of families. Chapter 5 provides a more complete description of how the components are configured in different types of programs.

As family literacy has evolved, these four components have become central to the effectiveness of family literacy programs. In a sense, these four characteristics allow us to define the lineage of family literacy programs, similar yet distinct from other intergenerational literacy efforts. Let us explore the importance and the reason for each component.

FAMILY LITERACY PROGRAMS PROVIDE DEVELOPMENTAL EXPERIENCES FOR YOUNG CHILDREN

Family literacy programs offer developmental learning experiences for the child, appropriately geared to the child's age. Such experiences are aimed not only at imparting skills but also at encouraging a lifelong love of learning. Family literacy involves more than just instruction; it is also

Family Literacy Programs: Four Examples

The four components of family literacy may be configured in a variety of ways. Programs differ in the comprehensiveness and level of intensity of services, the program location, the ages of children served, and the focus of adult education on the basic skills or English as a Second Language (ESL) instruction.

HOME-BASED

Wanda lives in a trailer in a remote rural area with her six children. Since the children's father left, she has been very discouraged and suffers from low self-esteem. Thanks to the home-based program sponsored by the county schools and the Community Action Agency, Wanda is visited every week for about 1 ½ hours. The home visitor works with her children, talks with Wanda about parenting concerns, and helps her see how she can help the children learn through play. The program will pay for transportation so that when the new baby gets a little older, Wanda can enroll in the local ABE program.

GROUP-BASED

Sherry is a young African-American woman who lives in an inner-city housing project with her two preschool-aged children. She attends a program that is jointly sponsored by the Housing Authority and the public schools. She rides the school bus to her local elementary school three full days each week where all four program components are offered each day. She is studying for her GED and likes the group lessons and individual study period, which are scheduled daily.

GROUP-BASED, ESL FOCUS

Lue is an Asian immigrant with three children who lives in a large city and attends a program that is located at a community college. He wants to improve his English so he can get a job and support his family. He and his four-year-old son attend the program four mornings a week. Lue enjoys the support of the group as he learns the language and culture of his new country.

COMBINATION

Vicky is a battered wife with four children. When her husband left her she was pregnant with her fifth child. Since Vicky cannot manage to attend school now, the program sends a home visitor once a week for about two hours. The home visitor helps Vicky to set goals and shows her how to work and play with her children. She is encouraging Vicky to prepare for the transition to the group where she will go to adult education class and parent group once a week while her children are in kindergarten, preschool, and infant care. Home visits will continue twice a month.

designed to deal with perceptions and attitudes toward learning. Family literacy first
and foremost helps the children in participating families prepare themselves to succeed in
both school and later life.

*Family literacy programs
provide developmental
experiences for young
children as well as adult
learning opportunities.*

While many programs address the early
developmental and educational needs of chil-
dren, family literacy combines early childhood learning with adult learning. Family literacy programs specifically support and encourage
parent-child interactions to promote greater understanding, communication, and skill gains.

Family literacy programs have also adopted the developmental approach to early childhood education, stressing the natural development of
children rather than "teaching" young children or treating them as smaller
versions of older children. Developmentally appropriate learning is another characteristic of excellent family literacy programs.

FAMILY LITERACY PROGRAMS PROVIDE BASIC SKILLS INSTRUCTION TO THE CHILDREN'S PARENTS OR PRIMARY CAREGIVERS

Parents participating in family literacy programs are motivated to learn perhaps more than at any previous time in their lives. Parents want to improve their literacy not only to help their children but also to improve their economic prospects once their children are in school. As a result, family literacy stresses appropriate literacy instruction for adults, instruction both contextual and individualized. Through literacy improvements among parents, family literacy achieves its several goals of changing the way parents value education, enhancing the way parents feel about their ability to influence the education of their children, helping parents feel good about their ability to be effective parents, and ultimately, improving the readiness of children while increasing the skills of adults.

An essential part of family literacy is to help family members relate more successfully and to build self-esteem by learning together.

Family literacy programs use adult literacy instructional techniques that are based on providing strong motivation to adults through contextual learning. Family literacy programs provide literacy and basic skills instruction that is directly related to the needs of adults in everyday life—in the home as well as in the workplace.

FAMILY LITERACY PROGRAMS WORK WITH PARENTS AND CHILDREN TOGETHER, HELPING THEM TO SHARE IN THE LEARNING EXPERIENCE

Family literacy advocates feel strongly that programs that serve only one part of the family—just children or only adults—miss an opportunity to reinforce learning gains and fall short of the ideal of family literacy. Although instructional programs for adults have demonstrated spillover benefits for children, for example, they usually cannot achieve the same results as a family literacy program that specifically provides instruction to both children and adults.

If parents gain literacy skills and children are better prepared for school but they don't learn how to learn together, the purposes of family literacy programs are not served. An essential part of family literacy is to help family members relate more successfully and to build self-esteem through learning together. As a result, most family literacy programs devote part of the program to activities that parents and children do together. For parents and children who often have very little experience in associating learning with family fun, this element of family literacy is extremely important.

Providing an opportunity for parents to learn better parenting skills even as they work with their children on learning and developmental experiences is a key part of the family literacy approach. Parents become better parents through practice, while children learn best in a supportive environment attended to by their parents.

FAMILY LITERACY PROGRAMS BRING PARENTS TOGETHER IN PEER SUPPORT GROUPS TO SHARE EXPERIENCES AND OVERCOME OBSTACLES TO FAMILY LEARNING

A host of obstacles may need to be overcome for the parent and child to benefit from the program. Parents may feel isolated and alone. They may have given up all hope and may fear change. The parents and children may

Parents supporting parents has become an essential part of family literacy.

not have the support of their spouses, significant others, or extended family members. They may experience such extreme poverty that they do not have the proper nutrition to stay healthy enough to be involved on a regular basis. Or they may be embarrassed that they do not have the proper clothing for themselves and their family. They may experience chronic crises, which they have little or no skills to deal with. Some parents may not have child care for younger children or they may not have transportation. Others may have had such negative experiences in school that the mere thought of returning to school may send them into a panic. A great deal of support is needed to make the courageous climb out of poverty and dependence.

As family literacy programs have matured and changed, program managers have found that bringing groups of parents together on a regular basis to develop support and encouragement can make a tremendous difference in the outcome of the program. Parents supporting parents has become an essential part of family literacy, an element that family literacy advocates believe cannot be neglected in family literacy programs.

Family literacy programs deal with the entire family. Although some programs focus only on the children or the parent-child interaction, family literacy strives to improve the lives of all the participants, parents and children alike. Experience has shown that most parents with low literacy skills also have damaged self-esteem. Just as children need high-quality developmental experiences to improve, so too parents must see their own skills and capabilities improving. As this occurs, they also need to learn how to improve their interaction with their children. Finally, all of the efforts can break down if the parents do not have an adequate support system. Over the years, family literacy practitioners have found that other parents provide the best support.

WHY WORRY ABOUT DEFINITIONS?

There are several reasons why we are careful to define family literacy in terms of the key elements of the program, rather than where the program takes place or the characteristics of parents or children. They include the following:

- *We want to be able to assess progress and judge the overall effectiveness of family literacy programs.*

Communities, state and federal policymakers, and financial supporters will be watching to see if this new approach is working. As the family literacy concept is being evaluated, it is important that programs implemented under the family literacy banner include the same components and address the same goals.

- *We want communities that implement family literacy to adopt a comprehensive program.*

As the idea of family literacy receives more support, other communities will want to start family literacy programs. The lofty but achievable goal of family literacy is to break the intergenerational cycle of low educational achievement that exists in many American families. We want the communities to have the best chance to attain this goal of family literacy. To do this, all components must be in place. Communities cannot expect to achieve the lofty goal of family literacy programs while only providing services that merely address aspects of the problem.

> • *We hope that as state and national policies direct resources to family literacy, they will target programs that are most likely to work.*

Like communities, state and national leaders who are beginning to direct substantial resources toward family literacy are watching closely to see whether these programs work. As we will see in Chapter 4, we have reason to believe that family literacy programs with these four elements are the most likely to succeed. Consequently, staying focused on this definition will help ensure that parents and children are best served and that the family literacy movement continues to attract resources as a wise public investment.

> • *We want the energies of the family literacy movement to stay focused on helping those with low skills, who are poor and often dependent.*

Too often, a promising idea with a catchy title becomes so fashionable that people call whatever they are doing by that name, and the focus of the idea is lost. Family literacy is first and foremost focused on helping people who have few resources to help themselves but whose lives can be changed through education. If we allow our attention to be diverted toward other objectives or a subset of our objectives — even though they are laudable — we risk losing our focus on people who can least help themselves.

RELATED INTERGENERATIONAL APPROACHES

Intergenerational family literacy efforts may not include all four elements but may still make valuable contributions to the literacy of family members. They include, for example, library-based family reading programs that encourage parents to read to their children. These programs focus on instilling a love of reading in children and encourage parent-child interaction. Although they lack the adult instructional and peer support components and they are not as intensive as family literacy programs, their value is in encouraging good reading habits among children, instilling a love of books, and familiarizing children with the library.

Other effective programs related to family literacy focus on adult literacy skill improvement and assume that the benefits of adults achieving better basic skills will be passed on to the children at home. Many of these programs teach parenting skills and provide peer support groups. In this way, they address several of the goals of family literacy programs and are showing intergenerational results even though instruction for children or the designated time for parents and children together are not part of the programs. As Tom Sticht, President, Applied Behavioral and Cognitive Sciences, Inc., has demonstrated, programs that work primarily with adults—such as the Wider Opportunities for Women program—do have a positive effect on their children's performance.

Similarly, programs such as Parents as Teachers and home-based Head Start programs may characterize their activities as promoting family literacy. While these programs are extremely valuable in their own right, they usually focus primarily on improving the development of the children, with some parent education. They do not focus on providing literacy instruction for the parents.

Programs such as these are extremely important and are often very successful in helping parents and their children. These programs form a very important part of the tapestry of services that have sprung up to address the economic and social needs of families and children. These programs stand together with family literacy as approaches toward eliminating intergenerational poverty and dependency. However, family literacy programs may hold the greatest promise of effectiveness because they begin with the premise that educating parents and helping them develop positive attitudes about their ability to learn is the critical first step to ensuring that their children will also become confident learners and that the cycle of illiteracy will be broken. [2]

ENDNOTES

[1] Sharon Darling, Testimony to the U.S. Senate Subcommittee on Education, Arts and Humanities on "The Challenge of Eliminating Illiteracy," May 18, 1989, p. 4.

[2] For a more extensive discussion of various intergenerational literacy programs, see Ruth Nickse, *Family and Intergenerational Literacy Programs* (Columbus, Ohio: Center on Education and Training for Employment, 1990).

Chapter 3

THE HISTORY OF FAMILY LITERACY

The history of families learning together is the history of literacy itself, but as a public policy family literacy's history is relatively short. The roots of the idea lie deep in the American democratic belief in universal literacy and education as the way out of poverty. Family literacy's most recent manifestation as public policy began less than a decade ago, and it is still evolving.

THE ROOTS OF FAMILY LITERACY

The idea that adults and children can learn together has roots in the early history of the family, when that was the way most children learned and many adults sharpened their skills. Adults have long known that you don't really understand something until you are able to explain it to a child. Children learn most of what they will ever know in the years before they go to school; most learning occurs within the family. For centuries, adults and children learned many of the skills they needed together. Often, these skills were learned from older adults.

25

The idea of family literacy also has its roots in the age-old motivation of parents helping their children learn. Family literacy builds upon the nearly universal desire of parents to express love for their children through teaching them as best they can. Children often bring new awareness among parents of the importance of education.

Family literacy also has roots in the long-standing desire of people to break the cycle of poverty and dependency that seems to be passed down from generation to generation in America. For most of human history, poverty and dependency have been accepted as a natural part of life for at least some people in any society. Only recently have people in Western industrial societies come to believe that poverty is not inevitable and that continuous progress is possible through educational achievement.

FAMILY LITERACY AND PUBLIC POLICY: KENTUCKY'S PACE PROGRAM

Despite the simplicity and power of the idea, the appearance of family literacy as a state or national policy thrust is relatively new. Some of the seeds for family literacy policy were planted as long as 30 years ago in Pennsylvania by now-Congressman Bill Goodling when he served as a school superintendent. Others were found in scattered local programs that stressed the family's role in early childhood education. But the several streams of thought were not put together in a coherent way until about 1985, when Sharon Darling, together with Jeanne Heberle, Coordinator of Early Childhood Education, Roger Noe, State Representative, and others in Kentucky began the first tentative steps toward a national family literacy movement.

In 1985, Assemblyman Roger Noe and Sharon Darling, then director of adult education for the Kentucky Department of Education, put together the elements of a new program entitled PACE—Parent and Child Education. As Chairman of the House Education Committee and as a former college student who read to children in homes in the Appalachia area of Kentucky, Noe was convinced that parental involvement in early childhood education was the key to educational success, but in Kentucky many parents lacked the literacy to encourage their children to learn, he felt.

For her part, Sharon Darling was frustrated by the failings of the school system that she and her colleagues in the adult education division had to try to repair: "We were getting nowhere in trying to remediate, when we should have been getting to the root of educational deficiencies and poverty. Looking to the family as the solution to the cycle of illiteracy rather than the problem would be the first step. As educators we knew we needed to help the most poverty-stricken, undereducated families replace the legacy of failure that was handed down to their children with a tradition of success by helping the parents themselves learn and pass that learning and the positive value of education on to their children. We decided to bring the parents and children together and help them learn."

According to Sharon Darling, the PACE program was begun to solve problems that were apparent as barriers to breaking the cycle of low literacy in areas of the state with the most pervasive illiteracy problems. These included areas where 70 percent of the adult population did not have a high school diploma and 70 percent of the children who entered school were not successful and dropped out before completing high school graduation. The problems that were encountered in implementing the PACE program were many: schools wrote children off the day they entered because of their family's poverty. Distance was a barrier for adults to participate in adult education programs. Low-literate parents themselves had a negative attitude about schools because of bruising experiences they encountered there. Their children were at great risk of failing from the first day. Schools were unprepared to accept the role of parents as important contributors to their children's education. Parents had no help for their own problems — nowhere to turn for resources or support from other families in similar situations. The PACE program set about trying to solve those problems, break down those barriers, and replace the barriers with incentives.

PACE was funded by the Kentucky legislature in 1986 and pilot programs were initiated in 6 rural counties. The following year, the legislature expanded the program to 18 rural counties. PACE brought together the strands of adult literacy, early childhood development, and parental support into a single package.

PACE provided parent literacy training in basic language, math skills, social studies, and preparation for the high school equivalency test. Adults took parenting courses and participated with their pre-school children in learning experiences, such as reading books. Parents and children shared meals and playtimes during the day. In most cases, PACE program activities took place in the schools, introducing both adult literacy and preschool activities into the school environment.

From its inception, it was clear that the PACE idea worked. Seventy percent of the adults in the program either received GED diplomas or raised their scores on standardized reading tests by two grade levels. Preschool children involved in the program were clearly better prepared for kindergarten and first grade, according to their teachers. Although critics sometimes pointed out that the families were self-selected and

therefore atypically motivated, PACE supporters were able to point to real successes in deeply economically distressed areas of rural Kentucky, a hard place to measure any progress.

Thomas S. Kenan III was instrumental in funding the expansion of family literacy in the nation.

PACE gained national attention in September 1988, when the Ford Foundation and Harvard University's Kennedy School of Government named it one of ten outstanding innovations in state and local government. This recognition spurred the creation of new programs modeled after it.

THE KENAN PROJECT

During the late 1980s, the William R. Kenan, Jr. Charitable Trust of Chapel Hill, North Carolina, had taken an interest in PACE. In January 1988, it provided a major grant to establish model family literacy programs at

three sites in Louisville, Kentucky, and four counties in North Carolina.

According to Thomas S. Kenan III, "We never expected the William R. Kenan, Jr. Charitable Trust to get involved in family literacy, but it just happened in a very wonderful way. Mr. Friday and I heard about the program when we visited Secretary William Bennett in Washington and asked what the most creative work was in the field of literacy at the current time. Secretary Bennett encouraged us to take a trip to Kentucky, and when we left we were convinced this was something that would really break the cycle of low literacy. We were committed to exploring the expansion of this exciting program and to conducting research as we took the program to urban areas and to other states."

The Jefferson County school system was selected to administer the Kenan projects in Kentucky; in North Carolina, arrangements for joint administration were made between local school systems and state-funded community colleges.

For these Kenan projects, the original PACE model was modified slightly. More time was found each day for parents and children to be together; parents were required to volunteer at the schools; teacher training was extended; and a career education component was included in the adult literacy classes.

The Kenan project stressed parental support groups and provided intensive training for provider staff. Project directors also developed extensive management training programs for family literacy providers. A preschool curriculum based on the High/Scope experience was implemented. Literacy instruction techniques were improved and evaluative techniques stressed. In two years, a new and more sophisticated model for family literacy programs emerged. Through the development of this model, the four elements now recognized as essential to any family literacy program were refined.

Over 300 families participated in the first two years of center-based model programs in Kentucky and North Carolina. Early evaluations of these programs showed unequivocally that the program worked. Follow-up studies on about a quarter of the families showed that children who participated in these Kenan-funded programs were succeeding academically in the early elementary grades. They had higher than expected self-confidence and motivation. Their teachers had positive attitudes toward them and predicted that the children would continue to succeed in school.

Parents who participated in the Kenan project were found to be supportive of schooling and were more likely to volunteer to work in the school. An early evaluation of parents completed after the first year of the project showed that parents, too, had gained literacy skills and self-esteem. At the end of the first year, most parents had gained at least two years in grade-level-equivalent reading skills, and their attitudes toward education had also improved.

The Kenan project provided the knowledge and experience necessary to convince others that family literacy was not just a good idea but that it could work on a national scale. By investing in pilot projects in Kentucky and North Carolina, the William R. Kenan, Jr. Charitable Trust had laid the foundation for a new institution, one that could help lead a nascent family literacy movement.

THE NATIONAL CENTER FOR FAMILY LITERACY

Because the pilot projects were successful and because the Kenan project office was deluged with requests — more than 5,000 from across the country — for information about the project and about family literacy, the Kenan Charitable Trust elected in April 1989 to broaden the scope of the project and to expand its staff. Three months later, the National Center for Family Literacy was established in Louisville, Kentucky, with a grant from the Kenan Trust to provide funds to support the Center's first year of operations.

The mission of the National Center for Family Literacy is to promote family literacy programming and to see it implemented effectively across the nation. To achieve this mission, the National Center

- Provides training and assistance to state and local leaders who become interested in launching family literacy initiatives — helping them develop programs that work and policies to encourage and sustain those programs
- Offers staff development and technical assistance workshops that enable educators engaged in designing and operating family literacy programs to benefit from the

31

experience of past family literacy efforts and the expertise of recognized leaders in family literacy

- Conducts demonstration projects and publishes research to document and advance the state of the art in family literacy programming — testing new instructional methods and documenting carefully what works and what doesn't work in family literacy

- Continues to spread the word about family literacy — using speeches, newsletters, and reports to ensure that family literacy is not forgotten in the vicissitudes of the public policy process, that it remains at the top of the public policy agenda at the federal, state, and local levels[1]

Since opening its doors in July 1989, the National Center has assisted thousands of educators and policymakers throughout the nation in developing quality family literacy programs (see sidebar listing of the organization's key events on p. 33). Its activities have been concentrated on training family literacy providers, working with states and communities to help them start family literacy programs, and developing national support for community family literacy initiatives.

Its most visible effort has been the Toyota Families for Learning Project (see "The Toyota Families for Learning Program" sidebar on p. 35). Since 1991, the Toyota Motor Corporation has provided over $5.1 million to support family literacy programs in major cities throughout the United States. First-round funding in the Toyota program went to family literacy projects in Atlanta, Pittsburgh, Richmond, Rochester, and Tucson. Second-round funding went to Seattle, Dallas, St. Louis, Ft. Lauderdale, and New Orleans. A new round of funding will add five cities by fall of 1993. In addition to establishing family literacy programs throughout the country, the Toyota Families for Learning Program has encouraged the development of collaborations in each participating city. The collaborative partners include public agencies, private businesses, and civic organizations, which provide funding and services to the program. This community investment insures the longevity of the program long after initial funding ends. The National Center for Family Literacy is also working with other companies, such as Minolta, Apple Computer

National Center for Family Literacy—
A Short History of Events

DATE	EVENT
1988	Kenan Trust funds family literacy project in seven sites to develop model family literacy programs in North Carolina and Kentucky and to conduct research on those programs.
1989, July	National Center for Family Literacy established with funds from Kenan Trust beginning Kenan's long-term commitment to the expansion of family literacy nationwide.
1989, Aug.	NCFL inaugurates major training and technical assistance program.
1989, Nov.	Apple Partnership begun with $250,000 worth of Apple computers and linkages through AppleLink.
1991, Jan.	NCFL and Toyota announce $2 million "Families for Learning" challenge grant program.
1991, Feb.	NCFL and Parents as Teachers National Center join in a partnership to develop a model serving children aged 5 and younger on Indian reservations.
1991, March	NCFL and Toyota announce support of family literacy projects in Atlanta, Pittsburgh, Richmond, Rochester, and Tucson.
1991, Aug.	NCFL announces long-term results of evaluation research that shows effectiveness of family literacy model, especially for children.
1991, Sept.	Apple awards additional $310,000 in computer equipment to Toyota Families for Learning Program.
1992, Feb.	Toyota provides an additional $1.6 million for family literacy programs.
1992, April	NCFL sponsors first national conference on family literacy, with over 500 participants around the nation.
1992, May	NCFL and Toyota announce support of family literacy projects in Dallas, Seattle, St. Louis, Ft. Lauderdale, and New Orleans.
1993, Feb.	Toyota announces grant of $1.5 million to expand Toyota Families for Learning Program to five additional cities.

Source: National Center for Family Literacy

Inc., Coca-Cola, and Spiegel, to funnel support to community family literacy efforts.

Perhaps the Center's most effective activity has been the training and program development support for hundreds of family literacy programs nationwide. In its short history, the National Center has provided policy and administration workshops for over 2,000 people from 47 states. Week-long training programs for staff implementing family literacy programs have been attended by over 3,000 people from all 50 states. In all, the Center has helped start over 900 family literacy programs around the country.

The National Center's approach to family literacy offered a sorely needed resource for states and communities. As Sue Berg, Coordinator of the Governor's Council on Literacy for the State of Hawaii, put it: "Hawaii researched several different (literacy program) models. Hawaii's literacy leaders, including First Lady Lynne Waihee, sought a model which was based on a family-strengthening philosophy and could be adapted to Hawaii's diverse people. Our intent was to find a model which included an evaluation component and a training component. We intended to find the best model — truly the thoroughbred of family literacy. These programs are propelling us toward our goal of a literate Hawaii."

The Center has shepherded family literacy from the seed of an idea to the flower of a movement in just a few years. It has clarified the essential elements of family literacy and helped programs across the country combine these elements in ways that fit with their local needs and resources. It has assumed the role of midwife to the family literacy movement.

EVEN START

Even as the family literacy movement was beginning through the extension of the PACE programs to the Kenan Family Literacy Project, other voices were heard supporting the concept of family literacy. Foremost among those voices was that of Congressman Bill Goodling, who had for many years shared the concern that education reform was missing an important family element. While he supported the highly successful Head Start program, he also had a vision of intergenerational learning that he championed in Congress beginning in the early 1980s. He envisioned a new program called Even Start (see sidebar on p. 37). He and other poli-

The Toyota Families for Learning Program

WHAT

The Toyota Families for Learning Program has grown from an idea in 1989, based on Kentucky's PACE program, to a major nationwide commitment to provide models of collaboration and cooperation for communities to improve family literacy. Three family literacy programs have been established in each of ten participating cities based on the Kenan Trust Family Literacy Model.

WHO

Funding is provided by the Toyota Motor Corporation in a grant to the National Center for Family Literacy.

WHY

The purpose of the grants is to increase the availability of family literacy programs to needy families across the country.

HOW

The Toyota Motor Corporation has helped to pave the way for the successful implementation of family literacy programs in midsized to large cities. A sponsor is identified in each participating city. The program encourages the participating cities to involve a variety of community agencies and organizations not only in the planning stages but throughout the project.

HOW MUCH

In 1991 Toyota made the single largest contribution to date to an intergenerational literacy program by donating $2 million to be divided among five cities. The program was expanded to five additional cities in 1992 with an additional $1.6 million granted by Toyota. An additional five cities will be added in 1993 with $1.5 million in new funding. Each participating city makes a commitment to secure additional funding to support the comprehensive program.

Source: National Center for Family Literacy

tical leaders believed that Even Start would enable parents as well as children to receive a better chance through education. They began to look for a vehicle to enact their ideas.

Their opportunity came in 1988 when the Even Start program was enacted as a demonstration program through the Hawkins-Stafford Elementary and Secondary Education Improvement Act. According to the law, the Even Start program is designed to

> ...improve the educational opportunities of the Nation's children and adults by integrating early childhood education and adult education for parents into a unified program... The program shall be implemented through cooperative projects that build on existing community resources to create a new range of services.[2]

The Even Start goals were similar to those of the PACE and Kenan programs. Under the Even Start programs, local education agencies, usually school districts, would provide an innovative combination of programs for adult basic education, parenting education, and early childhood education. The Even Start program expanded the PACE and Kenan programs, allowing for a broader age range, including children up to age seven. It also encouraged a home visitation component. The Even Start programs have three interrelated goals:

- To help parents become full partners in the education of their children
- To assist children in reaching their full potential as learners
- To provide literacy training for their parents[3]

Under the law, children aged one through seven who reside in an elementary school attendance area eligible for Chapter I compensatory education funds could be served, along with their parents.[4] Although the Even Start legislation required that at least some part of the program be home-based, center-based programs were also allowed. Federal funds would support 90 percent of program costs in the first year, declining to 60 percent in the fourth year of program operation. The Even Start law also required that the Secretary of Education undertake an annual independent evaluation and report to Congress by September 30, 1993, on the effectiveness of Even Start programs.

In 1989, Lauro Cavazos, the Secretary of Education, began to make discretionary grants averaging about $200,000 for Even Start projects all over the country, from Birmingham, Alabama, to Milwaukee, Wisconsin. By February 1992, 240 grants had been awarded, some for up to 4 years. Total spending on grants in the Even Start program grew to almost $50 million in 1991. The number of projects nearly doubled from 1990 to 1991.

What Is Even Start?

WHAT

Even Start, a federal program enacted in 1988, was designed to integrate early childhood education with adult education to improve the educational opportunities for children and adults. The success of the program was dramatic within the first three years of its implementation. During this time the number of Even Start programs doubled.

WHO

To be eligible for this program, a parent must need basic adult education, reside in a school attendance area that receives Chapter I funds, and have a child aged seven or younger. Local education agencies are the program providers.

WHY

Even Start addresses three interrelated goals: helping parents become full partners in the education of their children, assisting children in reaching their full potential as learners, and providing literacy training for their parents. Even Start grew out of a concern that education reform was missing an important family element.

HOW

Even Start programs are usually run by the local school district. Classes are mainly conducted within the setting of the classroom, but some programs actually take place directly inside the individuals' homes. The program's flexibility in meeting the needs of the individual families is a major element of its success.

HOW MUCH

For fiscal year 1992, Even Start grants totaled approximately $70 million. Approximately $200,000 was awarded to each Even Start program across the nation.

Source: The Even Start Act—H.R. 2535

Although Even Start programs have been operated by school districts, they adopt a broad range of techniques for improving literacy in low-income families. In New York City, for example, a combination of prekindergarten classes and mother-child reading programs was funded in Community School District 18. In Minneapolis, a center-based program similar to the Kenan project was funded, while in Broward County, Florida, a one and a half hour per week home visiting program was supported. While most Even Start programs include several of the components of family literacy, few include all four of these components in an intensive and comprehensive program. However, many of the programs are moving toward more comprehensive, intensive, integrated models. They are developing additional components as they mature and their methods and materials become more sophisticated.

The National Literacy Act of 1991 amended the Even Start Act to change its name to the Even Start Family Literacy Program. The new literacy law also established community-based organizations and other nonprofit organizations as eligible entities for grants and provided that a family's eligibility remains active until both the child and the parent are ineligible.

In addition, the Literacy Act established $75,000 as the minimum grant under the state grant program and allowed 5 percent to be used for administration and technical assistance. The Act also reserved 2 percent of the funds under the national program for technical assistance and evaluation.

In a major victory for family literacy, the new Literacy Act authorized $100 million in fiscal year 1992 and such sums as may be necessary in fiscal year 1993 to carry out the Even Start program. It also authorized $2 million for a contract with the Corporation for Public Broadcasting to develop and disseminate family literacy programming and related materials.

Adequate authorizations, however, do not always guarantee substantial appropriations. Nevertheless, Even Start funding has grown rapidly, a tribute to the attractiveness of the idea in Congress, the strong support from leaders of both the House and Senate — Congressman Bill Goodling and Senator Paul Simon — and support for family literacy by former First Lady Barbara Bush. Initial funding was set at $14 million. By 1991, Even Start funding had increased to $70 million, triggering a provision in the original law that when funding passed the $50 million mark, the program would be turned over to the states. As of 1992, the administration of the Even Start program is being shifted to the state level.

Even Start's initial funding has been a significant boost to the family literacy movement across the nation. In the first year of operation — October 1989 to May 1990 — approximately 2,800 families were served. By the second year of operation — June 1990 to May 1991 — 4,800 families were served. Six hundred and fifty of these families were continued from the first year of operation. For the third program year, it is estimated that more than 9,000 of these families received intensive and long-term services while others participated for a brief time and then dropped out. Data from the third year of operation will enable us to know how many families received the full benefit of the programs.

To date, 240 school districts across the nation have been chosen to develop these family-oriented parent and child programs. If funding for Even Start grows, as seems likely, this program will remain the most important source of funds for family literacy efforts, unless state governments invest in family literacy in a significant way.

THE BARBARA BUSH FOUNDATION FOR FAMILY LITERACY

Barbara Bush, thirty-eighth First Lady and a lifelong lover of books, became formally involved with literacy efforts when she knew

Barbara Bush brought national attention to the family literacy movement through her leadership in the Barbara Bush Foundation for Family Literacy. Here she talks with parents at a family literacy program in Louisville.

that her husband would run for high public office and that there would be an unparalleled opportunity for her to make a difference in this important area. As her understanding of literacy issues deepened, she began to look for a way to lend her prestige and support to a special area in the literacy struggle — family literacy.

On March 6, 1989, the Barbara Bush Foundation for Family Literacy (see sidebar on p. 41) was announced at a White House luncheon hosted by the First Lady. Expressing her conviction of the importance of family literacy, Mrs. Bush stated: "Sharing the pleasure of learning to read has to be one of the most important experiences a loving adult and child can have. Reading brings families together."

The mission of the new foundation was defined as follows:

- *To support the development of family literacy programs*—help mobilize the creativity, resources, and will of a country as great as America and make it possible to gain control of our literacy crisis and build a nation of readers by building families of readers.
- *To break the intergenerational cycle of illiteracy* — help provide settings where parents and children can learn to read together with materials and instruction available to each of them.
- *To establish literacy as a value in every family in America* — help every family in the nation understand that the home is the child's first school, that the parent is the child's first teacher, and that reading is the child's first subject.[5]

The Foundation established a governing board and a corporate support committee that to date has helped raise over half of a targeted $25 million endowment.

According to Benita Somerfield, Executive Director, three grant-making cycles have been completed for projects underwritten by the Barbara Bush Foundation for Family Literacy. In September 1990, eleven grants totaling $500,000 were awarded to community-based organizations, community colleges, universities, literacy programs, elementary schools, churches, and others. A second grant-making cycle was completed in 1991, expanding the number of grantees by 13 and awarding

The Barbara Bush Foundation for Family Literacy

WHAT

The Barbara Bush Foundation is an all-volunteer endeavor run by an eight-member board of directors. It is a fund of the Foundation for the Greater National Capital Region. Established on March 6, 1989, its mission is to support the development of family literacy programs, break the intergenerational cycle of illiteracy, and establish literacy as a value in every American family.

WHO

Any person or organization interested in information about family literacy can contact the Foundation. Grant applications come from a broad range of organizations including schools, community-based organizations, libraries, YMCAs, and churches.

WHY

The Foundation's main goals are to help break the intergenerational cycle of illiteracy and to establish literacy as a value in every home in America. Millions of Americans lack the literacy skills they need to function. Many are parents. This lack of skills severely limits the quality of their lives, their role in society, and the development of literacy skills of their children.

HOW

The Barbara Bush Foundation provides national recognition of successful programs, awards grants to help establish successful family literacy efforts, provides seed money for community planning of interagency family literacy programs, supports training and professional development for teachers, encourages recognition of volunteers, educators, and students, publishes and distributes materials that document effective working programs, and supports family reading.

HOW MUCH

The Foundation has set a goal of a $25 million endowment, which will provide approximately $1.7 million per year for grants and operating costs. To date, $1.5 million has been awarded to programs across the country.

Source: The Barbara Bush Foundation for Family Literacy

---

another $500,000. The third round of grants awarded in November 1992 totaled another $500,000 and went to 16 grantees.

The Barbara Bush Foundation for Family Literacy has focused its resources on helping communities start family literacy programs. An equally important contribution to family literacy has been the extensive publicity and public support that Barbara Bush and the Foundation have brought to the role of family reading in the educational and personal development of the child.

Early in 1989, the Foundation published *First Teachers: A Family Literacy Handbook for Parents, Policymakers, and Literacy Providers.* Twenty thousand copies have been distributed across the United States to organizations, public libraries, and individuals. *First Teachers* not only explains the fundamentals of family literacy but establishes Mrs. Bush's role as a leader in the movement.

First Teachers was also a way of showcasing many of the first and most promising family literacy programs. Besides the PACE and Kenan project programs, the book summarized the essential components of family reading and home-based programs such as the HIPPY program, MotherRead,® Parents as Partners, and other family-oriented reading programs.

In addition to the first book on family literacy, since 1991 the Barbara Bush Foundation has also distributed approximately 400,000 brochures entitled "Barbara Bush's Family Reading Tips." This brochure is part of a broader thrust by the Foundation to encourage literacy-related activities in all families. It is being distributed to schools, libraries, bookstores, federal agencies, and local Head Start programs and has done much to promote family literacy across the nation. A Spanish-language version became available in September 1992.

First Teachers and "Barbara Bush's Family Reading Tips" — together with the very visible leadership of Mrs. Bush — have enabled the Foundation to raise public awareness of the need for family literacy programs and the crucial role of parents in the development of their children's skills and love for reading. In this way, the Barbara Bush Foundation has been an important support for all family literacy programs and family reading initiatives.

THE BUREAU OF INDIAN AFFAIRS INITIATIVE

The Bureau of Indian Affairs has embraced family literacy efforts as part of its mission to provide quality education for American Indians and Alaska Natives from early childhood through life (see sidebar on p. 44).

Collaborations between the National Center for Family Literacy and the Bureau of Indian Affairs began in the spring of 1990. By November of that year, plans solidified to include family literacy using the PACE/Kenan Model, as part of the educational core in a limited number of Native American schools. The National Center for Family Literacy became a full partner with the Parents as Teachers National Center in St. Louis, Missouri, to design an educational program for families whose children ranged in age from birth to five.

Combining a home-based model with the center-based model created a new paradigm and necessarily brought about the need for a new training and technical assistance plan. With the structure in place and the training delivered, the First Native American Family and Child Education programs began on five reservations in January 1991.

Five more sites wrote proposals to the Bureau of Indian Affairs, participated in site evaluation, attended informational and training sessions, and began to implement family education programs in the fall of 1992. Plans are in place to increase the number of programs on Native American lands.

THE APPLE PARTNERSHIP AND FAMILY LITERACY

In the spring of 1990 Apple Computer, Inc., gave a boost to the use of computers in family literacy programs when it awarded $250,000 in computer equipment to the National Center for Family Literacy. In turn, the Center awarded equipment grants to five family literacy programs across the country. Since then, teachers and students in this Apple Partnership have been incorporating the computer as a literacy tool in their programs. Rather than utilize commercial programs that feature skill drills and practice activities, adult students have been encouraged to develop their basic skills by using the word processor, database, and spreadsheet applications. Using these applications has increased the students' sense of control in their academic work.

In the early childhood classrooms, three- and four-year-olds have used the computer to explore their environment through programs that emphasize the key experiences in their development. Parents and children together have designed computer-generated projects, played educational games, and talked together about the stories and pictures displayed on

43

The Bureau of Indian Affairs F.A.C.E. Program.

WHAT

The Bureau of Indian Affairs (BIA) Family and Child Education Program is designed to meet the educational needs of undereducated Native American parents and their children aged birth to five. The program integrates home-based and center-based early childhood and adult education components, reflecting the cultural traditions and values of each community. Five reservations piloted the program from January 1991 to August 1992; successes were dramatic. Five more sites began to serve families in September 1992. Training and technical assistance is provided by NCFL and Parents As Teachers.

WHO

To be part of this program the children of attending parents must be eligible to enter a bureau-funded school. Parents must need basic adult education and have children aged birth to five.

WHY

The purpose of the F.A.C.E. Program is to address the literacy needs of the family. The program also addresses the National Education Goals and Indian America 2000+. The office of Indian Education Programs' goal is to provide quality education for American Indians and Alaska Natives from early childhood through life.

HOW

F.A.C.E. programs are run by the local BIA or contract schools on Native American sites. Academics for adults are conducted on site in the homes. Parent and child interaction is a regular part of the school day, as is the Parent Group Meeting, during which a discussion of critical issues becomes the focus. Preschool on-site and home instruction are based on developmentally appropriate curricula.

FUTURE OF F.A.C.E

The office of the Indian Education Programs is planning to increase the number of family education programs in BIA-funded schools each year, as well as provide such programs to tribes without bureau-funded schools and tribal consortia as funds become available.

Source: National Center for Family Literacy

the computer screen. Students have used computers to advance their typing skills and have written resumes in preparation for obtaining jobs after completing the program.

AppleLink, Apple's telecommunications system, has connected participants who share activities, strategies, and concerns with each other regularly. In addition, the Center is able to respond to questions and gather data pertinent to the project via AppleLink. In the fall of 1991 Apple awarded an additional grant of $310,000 to the programs participating in the Toyota Families for Learning Program. Using the lessons learned by the original Apple Partnership participants, these programs have demonstrated the power of the computer as a literacy tool.[6]

HEAD START AND FAMILY LITERACY

In 1991, the Head Start program announced a Head Start Family Literacy Initiative (see sidebar on p. 47). In a document entitled "Promoting Family Literacy Through Head Start," the Head Start administration "calls upon every Head Start grantee to recognize family literacy which is clearly reflected in the regular activities of their Head Start programs."[7] Although

Computers are a powerful literacy tool for parents and children.

the exact methods of implementing this call are left to the local Head Start community, the Head Start program administration is clear about its goals:

- To enable Head Start parents to develop and use literacy skills which enable them to become more active and effective participants in the community, in the workplace, in their child's education and development, and in their efforts to obtain economic and social self-sufficiency.

- To enhance children's literacy development by helping parents become more effective as their children's "first teachers."[8]

Head Start program administrators are being urged to have a literacy program in place for families, a target set by the Commissioner of the Administration for Children, Youth and Families for 1992.[9]

More recently, Congress has sent to the President amendments to the Head Start enabling legislation that include requirements for Head Start programs "to provide (directly or through referral to educational services in the community) parents of children who will participate . . . with child development and literacy skills training in order to aid their children to attain their full potential."[10]

It is still too early to estimate the full effect of these directives emanating from Washington to Head Start programs around the country. No new funds were earmarked for the Head Start Family Literacy Initiative, and local programs are not required to take specific actions. It is fair to expect, however, that this initiative will provide a catalyst to thousands of Head Start programs around the country at least to look into the possibilities of using some of their growing resources to support family literacy components.

Family literacy advocates have been working with Head Start programs in many communities to form coalitions that will blend Head Start's new interest in family literacy into the mix at the local level. In South Carolina, for example, the National Center for Family Literacy has worked with Head Start leaders and program managers to develop a statewide strategy for family literacy. In Tucson, Arizona, the Pima County superintendent of schools was instrumental in combining Head Start and family

Head Start and Family Literacy

WHAT

The Head Start Program has initiated a Family Literacy Initiative to enable Head Start parents to enhance their literacy skills and their children's literacy development by helping parents become more effective as their child's "first teachers." H.R. 5630 has mandated the provision of literacy services directly or through referral by Head Start programs as well.

WHO

All Head Start program administrators are being encouraged to have a program in place by the end of 1992.

WHY

Head Start has long recognized the importance of parents as first teachers. Parental involvement in its preschool child development programs has been key to the success of Head Start. In order to maximize the development of social competence in the young children it serves, Head Start is beginning to incorporate a family-centered approach to its literacy programs.

HOW

Head Start programs have been in place for years and have developed a community identity as a place for learning. By extending the existing Head Start programs to include family literacy programs, adult learners can easily be recruited. The family-centered nature of the Head Start program may make it easier to retain adults as well. The basic premises of Head Start include parent involvement and empowerment through the activities of the program. Family literacy programs take this involvement one step further and allow parent and child to learn together through the use of the proven holistic child development methods used by Head Start.

HOW MUCH

Head Start program funds have increased substantially in recent years. Program administrators are encouraged to target some of these increases to family literacy.

Source: "Promoting Family Literacy Through Head Start," U.S. Department of Health and Human Services, Administration for Children and Families, September 1991.

literacy programs. In Hawaii, Leeward Community College has joined in a partnership with Head Start and the Department of Education. The (Makaha) 'Ohana Family Literacy Program began its third year of successful operation in 1992. In Dallas the Head Start program has joined with Dallas Can! Academy and the Dallas Independent School District to initiate a comprehensive family literacy program. More states and communities are sure to follow as Head Start programs around the country adopt family literacy as a key goal.

STATE INITIATIVES

From the beginning, state governments have played a significant role in family literacy. Washington was the first state to implement a comprehensive approach to this issue. They put in place a statewide program resembling Even Start in the mid-1980s. The first family literacy programs containing all four elements were begun by the commonwealth of Kentucky, and state officials were active in supporting the extension of the center-based model programs in North Carolina.

State officials have been intrigued with the family literacy concept because it promises to deal with several difficult problems facing state policymakers. State policymakers are facing rising costs for health care and welfare at the same time that spending for educational improvement is straining budgets. Strong efforts are being mounted to enhance economic development, in part through programs to upgrade the skills of the labor force. A program such as family literacy that addresses all of these issues at once has been perceived very positively, although only a few states have developed statewide initiatives.

Modeling their efforts after the Kenan programs in Kentucky and North Carolina, Hawaii, South Carolina, and Louisiana have taken significant steps to support family literacy. Illinois, New York, Florida, and California have begun to coordinate programs in order to stimulate family literacy. Other states, including Mississippi, Minnesota, and Arizona, have included family literacy in their comprehensive adult literacy plans, but have not yet taken action to implement statewide family literacy initiatives. All of these state efforts are supported with training and technical assistance from the National Center for Family Literacy.

State support for family literacy has taken many forms. Major legislation on family literacy passed in Hawaii in 1990 and Louisiana in 1991. Provisions for family literacy were enacted as part of the education reform package in Mississippi in 1990. In other states, major institutions have

Key Events in Family Literacy's Short History

DATE	*EVENT*
1985	Kentucky begins P.A.C.E. Program. PACE stands for "Parent and Child Education." First state to pass family literacy law.
1985	Congressman Goodling introduces first federal legislation supporting family literacy.
1986	Kentucky General Assembly funds two-year pilot PACE program in six rural counties.
1986	Hearings begin on Even Start program.
1988	Kenan Trust funds family literacy project in seven sites to develop model family literacy programs in North Carolina and Kentucky.
1988	Even Start program passes as part of the Hawkins-Stafford Elementary and Secondary School Improvement Act. Initial funding is about $14 million.
1989, March	Barbara Bush Foundation for Family Literacy organizes to provide advocacy, information, and resources for family literacy.
1989, July	Kenan Trust provides initial funds to create the National Center for Family Literacy.
1989, Sept.	Nation's governors and President announce six key education goals, including two that relate directly to family literacy.
1990, May	Hawaii becomes the second state to pass family literacy legislation.
1990, Sept.	Barbara Bush Foundation for Family Literacy announces first grants.
1991, January	NCFL and Toyota announce $2 million challenge grant program for family literacy programs in large cities.
1991, July	National Literacy Act passes, creating a National Institute for Literacy and making changes in Even Start program.
1991, August	Even Start appropriation raised to $70 million; states will gain control of programs as result of appropriation passing $50 million.
1991, Sept.	Head Start announces its "Family Literacy Initiative."
1991, Nov.	Barbara Bush Foundation for Family Literacy announces second round of grants.
1992, April	NCFL has established programs in all 50 states through training and technical assistance.
1992, April	First National Conference on Family Literacy held in Chapel Hill, North Carolina.
1992, July	Head Start amendments for family literacy passed by Congress.

embraced family literacy and worked for the creation of family literacy programs. In 1990, for example, the North Carolina Community College Board authorized its campuses to begin family literacy programs and research through funding from public/private partnerships as part of a challenge grant program with the Kenan Trust. In Illinois, an interagency group is helping family literacy programs, which now number over 100, get off the ground and grow. A more detailed description of how four different states — Hawaii, North Carolina, Louisiana, and Illinois — have addressed the issue of state family literacy policy is presented in Chapter 6: Developing a State Family Literacy Initiative.

It is too early to tell whether state support of family literacy will grow as fast as federal and community support of the concept. Only when states emerge from the economic recession and their fiscal crises ebb will we be able to tell whether they are seriously considering family literacy program strategies to reduce poverty and stimulate economic development.

SUMMARY: SIGNIFICANT CHANGE IN LESS THAN A DECADE

In less than a decade, family literacy has grown from a program supported by seed money to a national movement supported by federal legislation and policy directives. When the social history of the United States in this century is written, it may be that these few years in which family literacy contributed to the focusing of attention on the issues of intergenerational poverty are counted as a turning point. A timeline of key events in the family literacy movement to date is presented in the sidebar on page 49.

Family literacy is only now being translated from a concept into programmatic reality. As more and more communities consider investing in family literacy programs, they will want to know whether family literacy really lives up to its promises. What does the research say about family literacy? Does it work? The next chapter explores the research that begins to answer these questions.

ENDNOTES

[1] The National Center for Family Literacy, *Spreading the Word, Planting the Seed* (Louisville: The National Center for Family Literacy, 1991), 4.

[2] U.S. Department of Education, National Evaluation of the Even Start Family Literacy Program, First Year Report (Washington: Abt Associates, October 28, 1991), 1.

[3] Ibid, 2.

[4] U.S. Department of Education, *Federal Register, Part VII, Department of Education, 34 CFR Part 212, Even Start Programs; Final Regulations and Notice Inviting Applications* (Washington: U.S. Department of Education, March 23, 1989), 12142.

[5] "The Barbara Bush Foundation for Family Literacy" (Washington), 2.

[6] To receive information about the Apple Partnership, contact the National Center for Family Literacy (Publication: "Using Computers in Family Literacy Programs").

[7] U.S. Department of Health and Human Services, "Promoting Family Literacy Through Head Start" (Washington: U.S. Department of Health and Human Services, September, 1991), 7.

[8] Ibid, 2.

[9] Ibid.

[10] H.R. 5630, 102nd Congress, 2D Session, July 31, 1992.

Chapter 4

THE RESEARCH: HOW DO WE KNOW IF FAMILY LITERACY WORKS?

Family literacy is grounded in common sense. If we can provide good early childhood development experiences together with literacy instruction to children and their parents, these families ought to be able to build a better future. Through painful experience, however, we have learned that some ideas that seem intuitively true in theory turn out to be unworkable or simply wrong in the real world. It is important to examine the available evidence to determine if family literacy actually works and to identify any questions or concerns about the concept.

As programs develop in many communities across the nation, we will want to examine carefully the research available to us. Can we document whether family literacy works? Or, if we do not have iron-clad proof that family literacy works, what indications does the research give us about its probability of helping families? Do some elements or models of family literacy work better than others? Does the research suggest ways we might structure our family literacy programs to make sure they are most likely to succeed?

In this chapter, we will survey and summarize the results of research that gives us an indication about whether and how family literacy works. We will also explore a number of research questions relating to family literacy that are yet to be answered. Drawing on research from the more established fields of early childhood education and adult learning, we will attempt to draw lessons from that research to guide us when we consider developing family literacy policies and programs in our communities and states.

DIVIDING UP THE RESEARCH QUESTIONS

Since the field of family literacy itself is relatively new, it will be difficult to judge whether family literacy will achieve its goals based on specific evaluative research of family literacy programs themselves. While preliminary findings suggest that the Kenan Model and many Even Start programs are effective, we cannot base any firm conclusions about the field of family literacy on these results alone. To satisfy ourselves about

Research shows that adults do learn when given a "second chance," and they often learn faster than when they were children.

our research base, we need to divide the research effort into several discrete pieces, paralleling the four elements defining family literacy programs and exploring related questions. These might best be considered as questions:

- What are the benefits of early childhood development programs?

- What are the benefits of adult literacy programs?

- Are there benefits from parents and children learning together?

- Does peer support help parents?

- Is there evidence that programs that put these elements together can be more effective than other approaches?

- What do the early evaluations of family literacy programs show?

- What else do we need to know?

EARLY CHILDHOOD DEVELOPMENT

Early childhood development is a field that has generated a great deal of research. We know more about the effects of early childhood education than we do about many other fields of inquiry in social policy. Nearly all the research suggests that developmental experiences for preschool youngsters are beneficial, in both the short term and the long run. Even so, while the evidence of early childhood development programs' effectiveness is not conclusive, the research does suggest that strong early childhood development programs provide benefits especially to low-income children. We can only assume that these benefits will be magnified among children of families where literacy levels are very low, because early childhood development programs will provide the developmental stimulation that parents cannot easily provide if they are not literate.

Perhaps the most significant study of the effects of early childhood education was conducted by the High/Scope Educational Research Foundation in Ypsilanti, Michigan. As a result of the High/Scope Perry Preschool Project, some solid information is available about what happens to children when they are fortunate enough to participate in a high-quality early childhood education program. In this study, reported by David Weikart and his colleagues, groups of children who had received early childhood education experiences in preschool were compared to groups that had not. [1]

Established in 1962, the High/Scope Perry Preschool Project enrolled disadvantaged three- and four-year-old children in a half-day preschool program for eight months of the year. The mothers received a 90-minute

HIGH/SCOPE PERRY PRESCHOOL STUDY AGE 19 FINDINGS

■ Preschool Group

━ No Preschool Group

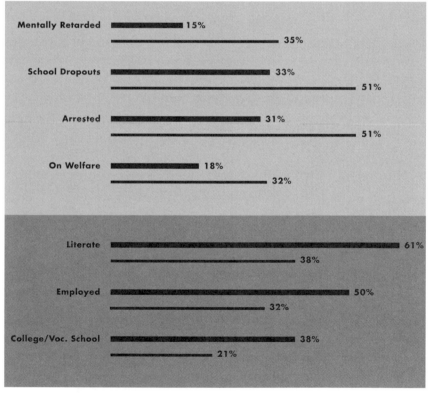

Mentally Retarded	15%	
	35%	
School Dropouts	33%	
		51%
Arrested	31%	
		51%
On Welfare	18%	
	32%	
Literate		61%
	38%	
Employed	50%	
	32%	
College/Voc. School	38%	
	21%	

Note: All group differences are statistically significant, p < .05, two-tailed.
Source: High/Scope Educational Research Foundation

home-teaching visit each week from the classroom teacher. The children selected for the study were randomly assigned to either the experimental group, which participated in the program, or to the control group, which remained engaged in the normal, though limited, processes typical of the home and community. Over the years a model curriculum was developed using Piagetian theory as the basis for the organization and delivery of the services. While the curriculum model has evolved, the essential components of the method have remained common to the work.

The results of the study have not varied over the years. The children who participated in the High/Scope Curriculum program demonstrated significantly higher scores on intelligence tests upon entry into regular school, though this advantage was lost by grade three. Performance on achievement tests has been higher in the preschool group since grade three. Teachers over the years have consistently rated the preschool group's performance higher.

By age 15 the original preschool group demonstrated a lower rate of self-reported juvenile delinquency. By age 19 the pattern of success for the preschool group was apparent in three major areas:

- In **education,** the preschool group graduated from high school in greater numbers; attended college or advanced training programs more often; and was less likely to be assigned to special education services during the school years.
- In the **world of work,** the preschool group was more likely to be both working and self-supporting.
- In the area of **social behavior,** the preschool group recorded less crime; less welfare use; and, if female, fewer teenage pregnancies.

Current and very preliminary follow-up data analysis of the study participants who have now turned age 28 suggest that the findings of performance of the group when they were age 19 will be again confirmed. If this is the case, the Perry Preschool study will be the first to show that children who received high-quality early childhood experiences benefit from those experiences throughout their early adult life.

The Perry Preschool findings are not the only information that indicates the value of early childhood education. In *Changed Lives*, Weikart and others summarize the results of seven controlled scientific studies that support the beneficial effects of preschool programs. In these studies, early childhood education experiences were provided to preschool children in programs that began operation in various years between 1962 and 1975. An average of 80 percent of the program participants—who ranged in age from 9 to 21 at the time of the studies — were located and interviewed. The results were summarized by Weikart and his coauthors as follows:

- **Early childhood** — improved intellectual performance
- **Elementary school** — better scholastic placement, improved scholastic achievement
- **Adolescence** — lower rate of delinquency, higher rate of high school graduation, higher rate of employment one year later [2]

Weikart notes that six of the seven studies indicate that "early childhood education can have an immediate and positive effect on children's intellectual performance."[3] Significantly, early childhood education reduced placement in special education classes by half. Three of the seven studies showed that early childhood education helped prevent children from dropping out of school, while several of the studies also indicated that scholastic achievement was increased. Finally, the Perry Preschool study indicates that early childhood education does seem to help prevent juvenile delinquency and prevent teen pregnancy.

Despite a popular misconception that the gains from early childhood education are lost by the mid-elementary grades, the evidence mounts that early childhood education works, the benefits stay with participants, and that benefits are both academic and social. But just any form of preschool day care does not result in these benefits. As Weikart and others point out, preschool experiences must be broadly developmental and include parental participation and competent leadership in order to benefit children in the long run. Family literacy programs can learn a great deal from the experience of early childhood development researchers that developmental preschool approaches work if we demand high-quality programs. Family literacy has the potential to help create a high-quality experience for preschoolers by getting parents involved who would not normally be involved in their children's education.

ADULT LITERACY

As difficult as it has been to demonstrate that early childhood education works, the research on adult literacy is distressingly thin. Because of years of work by people such as Tom Sticht, Larry Mikulecky, Hanna Fingeret, Judith Alamprese, Gordon Darkenwald, and others, we do have some clarity on a few issues in adult literacy—enough at least that we can advocate family literacy programs in good conscience. We therefore present a summary of what researchers do know about the effectiveness of adult literacy instruction, without tracking all of our conclusions to specific studies.[4]

ADULTS CAN MAKE SIGNIFICANT IMPROVEMENTS IN THEIR LITERACY SKILLS

Many adults who are potential participants in family literacy programs have doubted that they could ever learn to read, write, compute, or generally become more literate and able to function in society. The research shows that nearly every adult can improve her or his skills. Research on military literacy programs and many others has shown conclusively that adults do learn when given a "second chance," and that often they learn faster than when they were children. In fact, Sticht and others have estimated that when adults are motivated to learn and presented with materials in a context that has functional benefits to them, they can learn faster than traditional-age students in classroom situations.

To be sure, there is considerable doubt and controversy about how well literacy programs help adults to function or how long these learning gains stick with them. It also appears to make a considerable difference to adults what kind of skills they learn. Several studies have shown that general literacy advances do not necessarily transfer into job-related skill increases, for example. The research does show, however, that adults who are motivated to learn can make substantial advances in increasing basic literacy skills.

Adults need strong motivation and positive reinforcement to continue to exert the effort to improve their literacy skills over time.

ADULTS APPEAR TO LEARN IN DIFFERENT WAYS THAN CHILDREN

Once it is pointed out that adults might learn in different ways than children, it seems intuitively obvious. Yet far too many adult literacy programs have been operated on the assumption that adults are just children who failed to learn the first time they tried. In fact, adults process information differently from children. Perhaps because they have a larger language base from which to work, low-literate adults can often make more rapid progress in learning to read than children. The most effective adult literacy programs recognize that adults are not children and base their instructional practices on functional competencies that are useful to the adults.

Like children, however, adults learn best when instruction relates to everyday life and important roles, such as working outside the home or raising a family. Learning requires time, effort, and patience and is enhanced when opportunities are supplied to apply skills in adult functional settings. Learning may be accelerated when it is based on acquiring particular competencies. Adults who are allowed to move forward at their own speed are usually more comfortable. Adult learning is fastest when it is driven by strong motivation and where caring teachers provide individual attention and assistance.

ADULTS WHO ARE LEARNING ENGLISH AS A SECOND LANGUAGE
HAVE A DIFFERENT CHALLENGE FROM MOST LOW-LITERATE ADULTS

Adults who are seeking literacy in English as a Second Language (ESL) often are literate in their own language, and therefore learn in different ways from those who are not literate in their native tongue. In addition, ESL learners are usually strongly motivated and are willing to put in considerable time and effort, especially if instruction involves life skills and functional literacy.

ADULTS MUST BE STRONGLY MOTIVATED
TO MAKE A SUSTAINED EFFORT TO INCREASE LITERACY

Adults need strong motivations and positive reinforcement to continue to exert the effort to improve their literacy skills over time. Learning is neither easy nor inexpensive in time and effort. Adults have usually failed in school before and must overcome fear of failure. They have many other responsibilities and their time is often in short supply. Programs that do not address motivation in adults usually have very high attrition rates. Retention rates in most adult education programs are very low. If family literacy programs are to succeed in imparting skills to adults, they must address the issue of motivation.

PROGRAMS THAT PROVIDE A SUPPORT SYSTEM FOR ADULTS
APPEAR TO HAVE BETTER RESULTS THAN THOSE THAT DO NOT

Adults need more than just the opportunity to learn. They must also have some support in managing their family responsibilities, taking care of children, and with transportation and other day-to-day issues that raise obstacles to their success. Adult literacy instruction is best provided in the context of the daily lives of adults, and the more support they can receive from family literacy programs in their daily lives, the more effectively they will be able to learn.

These are a few things we do know about adult literacy. Later in this chapter we illustrate that there is much to discover about how adults learn and how to structure effective adult literacy programs.

In the context of adult literacy efforts, family literacy has several strong advantages in terms of what the research indicates probably works best. First, participants in family literacy programs are usually strongly motivated to learn. Mothers who are seeking to better themselves in front of their children have a strong motivation to "stick it out" and put in the effort to increase their skills. Second, family literacy programs provide strong support to the family. Child care, transportation, and peer support are all part of the family literacy recipe. Third, the context of literacy instruction is usually related specifically to the goals of the individual, either relating to parent-child learning or to employment. These three facets of family literacy programs comport well with what we do know about the most effective adult literacy programs.

There are other advantages to family literacy programs as well. Family literacy components are interrelated and reinforce each other, thereby making a comprehensive program rather than a fragmented one. Family literacy programs tend to have more comprehensive services from the community. Also, the commonality of age and interest of family literacy adult group members provides a basis for the group to come together more easily than in other adult literacy programs.

TIME TOGETHER

While there is no specific research on the question of whether the adult literacy and early childhood development experiences are improved when parents and children spend time together, there are strong suggestions in research that this is beneficial. In preschool programs, for example, the extent of parental involvement in the preschool is positively correlated with long-term benefits for children.

In family situations as well, we know that parents spending time with children in learning situations surely benefits the children and may also be helpful to the adults. In fact, the premise of several major programs, such as Head Start and Parents as Teachers, maintain that this experience is most beneficial to both parties.

Knowing that the best predictor of academic success is the educational level of the mother also strongly suggests that the success of parents in improving their skills influences the child's behavior, motivation, and school success. Making sure that parents and children spend time together learning in family literacy programs only makes sense in light of these findings.

PEER SUPPORT

In both the fields of adult literacy and early childhood development, program operators have long known that a supportive environment for program participants is an important part of making the educational components work. In Head Start, for example, parental involvement has been stressed from the beginning, and most research on Head Start points to the benefits of parental involvement in early childhood education. Programs such as Parents as Teachers and others focusing on parenting skills also are based on the premise that parental support is crucial for early development of children. When adult learners are supported and encouraged within their own communities and families, they work harder, learn more, and stay longer. Programs that provide education in isolation have the highest dropout rates, while programs that provide peer support appear to have the best records.

Based on these observations, the notion of peer support groups as part of family literacy was developed. When adult learners meet together, away from the children, they can discuss problems and opportunities and gain support from people engaged in similar struggles. The fact that peer support helps many people overcome difficulties relating to alcohol or drug abuse, for example, leads us to believe that support groups are effective in increasing the retention of adults in family literacy programs and in helping them solve problems.

PUTTING TOGETHER THE ELEMENTS OF FAMILY LITERACY

While we have reasonable evidence that each of the four components of family literacy appear to be effective in improving the lives of low-literate people and in helping their children break the cycle of dependency, we also have early indications that putting together these components may be synergistic, leading to a greater effect than just the sum of the parts. Dr. Andrew Hayes of the University of North Carolina, Wilmington, for example, has concluded that because the problems of families result from a variety of family sources, a program such as family literacy is most effective when it deals with multiple issues within the family, including not only undereducation but also parenting and attention to the development of young children. He also points out that significant changes in family behavior—in raising children and learning new skills—take a long time to take root. By combining a variety of program elements over a relatively lengthy period of time, family literacy programs maximize the chance for change to take root in the functioning of families over a long period of time.

Early results from family literacy evaluations are quite positive, indicating that families gain from combining the elements of family literacy programs. Evaluations conducted by Dr. Hayes and others conclude that when the four elements are put together, the behavior of families changes. Parents become more responsive to their children, children receive the developmental care they need, and families learn to work together more effectively. This suggests that family literacy programs will be the most effective when they take a balanced approach to all four elements of family literacy.

Some researchers suggest that the reason that family literacy appears to work well is that it takes as its focus the family itself. Increasingly, researchers into poverty and dependency and their relationship to families are identifying the barriers to economic and social success in terms of the entire family. As Heather Weiss, Director of the Harvard Family Research Project Center, has said: "Study after study has convinced us that we must focus on the whole family. Family literacy programs bring together early childhood development services for preschool youngsters, adult literacy instruction, peer support, and social services to families in a way that does something concrete for nearly every member of the family." While we do not have specific information that putting these types of programs together will work better than offering them separately, she says, "we have every reason to believe that family literacy programs are the ones most likely to work." [5]

The research indicates that the cost of family literacy is small compared to the costs of not providing services to break the intergenerational cycle of undereducation, poverty, and dependency. The first evaluations of family literacy have shown, for example, that far fewer students are repeating grades. The cost savings of preventing repeated grades alone would offset the costs of family literacy services, not even counting the longer term benefits to the child, school, and society. Long-term cost avoidance to society of early childhood development programs has been demonstrated, as has the effect of adult literacy programs on productivity among adults.

Because high-quality programs are required to make either early childhood development or adult literacy instruction work well, family literacy programs are not designed to cut corners on the provision of services. As Weikart and others have pointed out, simply providing a day care experience will not lead to benefits for children, whereas a broad array of developmental experiences will. Most researchers in adult literacy also believe strongly that contextually-based, professional instruction is more effective than volunteer tutoring of adults, however valuable that tutoring might be.

Nearly all the research in both early childhood development and adult literacy shows that supportive services, including access to a variety of social services, are sometimes required to make the educational components of the programs effective. All these services cost money, but if programs do not provide them, they are much less likely to be effective at all. There may be a critical level of resources that must be made available to a poor family below which they may be better off not becoming involved in a program at all.

While family literacy programs are not inexpensive, they have substantial advantages over more fragmented programs because family literacy programs deal with the family as a unit in a more holistic way than other approaches. Early results from evaluations of family literacy programs seem to indicate that these programs are well targeted and meeting many of their goals.

EARLY RESULTS FROM FAMILY LITERACY EVALUATIONS

Family literacy is so new that it is extraordinary that we have a track record as well-documented as we do. From the beginning, those who started or funded family literacy programs have expressed a belief in accountability and evaluation through the allocation of resources to data collection and assessment. This is true for all programs sponsored by Even Start, the Kenan Trust, the Toyota Motor Corporation, and the Barbara Bush Foundation. As a result, unlike most other social programs, we have a structure designed to generate information we can use to evaluate and fine-tune family literacy programs. The National Center for Family Literacy has sponsored a number of evaluations of programs, including the Kenan Trust programs, PACE in Kentucky, and the Toyota Families for Learning projects. In addition, we have the early results from the Even Start evaluation. The Even Start study was based on information from about 2,800 families in 73 programs and was conducted in late 1991.[6] The National Center for Family Literacy studies were based on information from 14 Kenan model programs and from Toyota Families for Learning programs at 15 sites in five cities. These evaluations were conducted in 1991 and early 1992 based on data from programs beginning as early as 1986.[7]

In the spring of 1991, the National Center for Family Literacy published a summary of what happens when family literacy programs serve undereducated parents and children. Based on all its evaluations, the Center concluded that family literacy programs:

> • *Increase the developmental skills of preschool children to prepare them for academic and social success in school.*

In both the Kenan and PACE programs studied, for example, teachers and parents both rated children who had participated in family literacy programs as significantly better prepared for school than they otherwise would have been. Virtually none of the children served had to repeat a grade, and as late as the fifth grade, children who had participated in family literacy programs were performing well.

> • *Improve the parenting skills of adult participants.*

All the evaluations indicated that parents felt that they were better equipped to be good parents. Program staff also rated nearly all parents as showing "some" or "much" improvement in parenting skills.

> • *Raise the educational level of parents of preschool children through instruction in basic skills.*

Most of the students in family literacy programs either passed the GED test or parts of it, pursued further higher education, returned to high school, or reported learning new skills that they felt would be useful on a job. Students who did not achieve their educational goals did not do so because they moved away or because of interference by a spouse or significant other.

> • *Enable parents to become familiar with and comfortable in the school setting and provide a role model for the child showing parental interest in education.*

Among those programs that were school-based, this goal was achieved for most parents. The evaluations indicate that many parents are becoming active volunteers in school and most have become actively involved in their children's homework. In all the National Center for Family Literacy evaluations, the vast majority of family literacy teachers rated their students as improved in terms of being better role models for their children. Over 40 percent had attained "much improvement" as role models, according to family literacy program providers.

> • *Improve the relationship of the parent and child through planned, structured interaction.*

Parents in general felt that they were better able to understand the needs of their children. Parents and children reported that they were working together on school-related activities at home or while riding the school bus. One evaluation stated that "there is much evidence that literacy has become a more important concept in many homes which previously did not give it much priority."[8]

> • *Help parents gain the motivation, skills, and knowledge needed to become employed or to pursue further education and training.*

Virtually all participants in family literacy programs studied by the National Center for Family Literacy listed as a goal either pursuing a job or further education at the conclusion of their work within family literacy. Single parents with small children contemplated going to work as soon as the children entered kindergarten. Most parents have identified the additional education they will need to get a job or improve their job prospects.

These results were reported in 1991 by the National Center for Family Literacy, based on its extensive evaluations and experience in working with hundreds of family literacy programs.

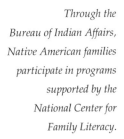

Through the Bureau of Indian Affairs, Native American families participate in programs supported by the National Center for Family Literacy.

From both the Even Start evaluations and the National Center for Family Literacy evaluations combined, we conclude that family literacy programs have significant impacts from a public policy point of view. Here are some of the findings from these evaluations.

FAMILY LITERACY PROGRAMS SERVE PEOPLE WITH SIGNIFICANT ECONOMIC, SOCIAL, AND EDUCATIONAL PROBLEMS

From its inception, family literacy has been aimed at breaking the cycle of dependency and poverty through education of both parents and children. It is important, then, to see whether family literacy programs in practice are attracting poor families with significant problems, or whether they are "creaming" — skimming off the most able people who have the fewest problems. Both the Even Start and the National Center for Family Literacy evaluations showed that family literacy programs are serving the groups of people they are intended to serve.

Over 70 percent of Even Start families had incomes under $10,000. Nearly four in five had not completed high school. Forty percent of participating adults were single parents. About half reported that government assistance was their primary source of support. About 82 percent of adult participants were female. Nearly 40 percent were white; 35 percent, black; 15 percent, Hispanic; and 7 percent, Native American.

68

The economic and educational problems reflected in this description of Even Start families clearly indicate that the program is serving those who are in dire need of such services. Families enrolled in programs sponsored through the National Center for Family Literacy relate similar statistics.

Actually, participants in the Kenan Trust model sites were reaching an even more disadvantaged population. Over 90 percent of parents were unemployed, and two thirds were receiving public assistance. Nearly three quarters had annual incomes below $7,500. Sixty-five percent were single-parent families, and over three-quarters were under the age of 30.

In the first round of the Toyota Families for Learning Program, which is targeted at families in large cities, nearly 60 percent of adults were black, 20 percent white, and 18 percent Hispanic. Over 70 percent of enrollees were in families where the mother was single. All parents dropped out of school before graduation, but over half made it through tenth grade. Ninety-six percent were unemployed and 85 percent had incomes of less than $7,500 per year. Seventy-seven percent relied on public assistance as the primary source of support.[9]

While people participating in family literacy programs are usually self-motivated, family literacy programs are reaching very poor people who face substantial educational and social obstacles. Many come into the program referred by JOBS and other welfare programs. Other parents are assigned to programs by the court for reasons of child abuse and neglect.

FAMILY LITERACY PROGRAMS HELP FAMILIES WITH MANY PROBLEMS RELATED TO LACK OF EDUCATION AND POVERTY

A key preliminary finding of both studies is the extent to which families participating in family literacy programs require and use supportive services. The Kenan Trust Model programs reported extensive problems in addition to the lack of literacy skills among parents. Over 80 percent of programs reported that parents had a variety of economic difficulties, such as lack of transportation or credit, as well as relationship or marital problems or trouble attending programs because of interference from family members.

While the Even Start preliminary data did not record problems of adults, it did indicate that adults in Even Start programs used support services extensively to try to solve some of their nonliteracy difficulties.

Transportation, mental health services, counseling, nutrition, health care, and many other support services were provided directly or through referral by more than half of the Even Start family literacy programs.

IN FAMILY LITERACY PROGRAMS PROVIDING ALL FOUR
PROGRAM COMPONENTS, CHILDREN ARE GAINING REAL BENEFITS

Perhaps the most significant and exciting findings of the preliminary assessments of the Kenan project are that children are performing above expectation in school as a result of their family literacy experiences. Based on interviews with parents and teachers of 79 children participating in Kenan project programs from 1988 to 1990, the National Center for Family Literacy found that children are exceeding expected performance in academics, motivation to learn, relations with other students, attendance, behavior, and self-confidence. Over 85 percent of students are judged by their teachers as likely to succeed in school, and 90 percent of children were *not* considered at risk for school failure by the teachers.[10]

It is important to compare these figures with what is likely to happen without this type of intervention. Children who live in homes with parents who don't have a high school diploma and those from economically deprived homes are five to six times more likely to drop out of school later in life. Fifty percent of these children are likely to be in the bottom 25th percentile of their class in terms of academic achievement. Fifty percent are likely to be retained in grade before grade four. Preventing a child from dropping out of school can mean enormous direct savings in welfare and social support programs and increased productivity. By preventing a child from repeating a grade or needing remediation, significant costs can be avoided. Educating a child costs well over $5,000 per year and the cost of remediation is an additional $3,000 per child per year. Savings can also result from avoiding placement in special education classes.

Results indicate that only 25 percent of children in family literacy programs required Chapter I or special education services and that none of the children who participated in family literacy programs had failed a grade. While these data are not conclusive, they suggest strongly that the early childhood education experiences of children in family literacy programs are paying off in better school experiences, direct cost savings, and significant cost avoidances.

PARENTS ARE PARTICIPATING IN AND SUPPORTING THEIR CHILDREN'S EDUCATION

Even though all the parents studied were high school dropouts themselves, many were serving as volunteers in their children's elementary schools. Teachers also consistently rated parents as supportive of their children's education in elementary school. According to the study, "parents reported that as a result of participating in the family literacy program they felt more comfortable talking to school personnel, were active participants in the local PTA, attended more school and community activities, spent more time helping children with their homework, and were spending more 'quality time' with their children."[11]

This family's participation in a family literacy program netted a GED and job for the mother and a better chance at academic success for her son.

One parent in a Kenan family literacy program remarked, "I'm secretary for the PTA. I am a parent consultant for Chapter I. I've helped the counselor in the office with paperwork, making sure the addresses and phone numbers of the children were correct. I've just finished helping my son's kindergarten teacher give [standardized] tests and I'm parent representative for the learning choice schools."

In addition, parents' self-concepts and self-esteem have been observed to improve over the course of the family literacy programs. This finding is supported by a great deal of anecdotal evidence given by program participants about their improved view of themselves. Parents reported a nearly unanimous improvement in self-confidence. Many parents indicated that they experienced significant changes in their lives as a result of passing a GED test, going back to school, learning new skills, or getting a job. One participant remarked: "When I first came here, I was only interested in getting my GED, that was it. Then, as the program went on, I thought, why stop here? So, I figured if I get the GED, then I'll go on [to community college]." In a significant finding, the National Center for Family Literacy studies showed that parents who had learned new skills were interested in further training, but needed help in finding it.[12]

Based on these studies, we can conclude that existing family literacy programs are recruiting the people they were intended to serve, that children are performing better in school, and that adults are participating in the education of their children more often and feel better about themselves. Although it is too early to draw final conclusions, evaluations of family literacy programs suggest that these programs are providing the benefits they promise.

RESEARCH FOR THE FUTURE OF FAMILY LITERACY

The amount of evaluative research on family literacy programs or their precursors is still too small to make sweeping conclusions about the efficacy of the program or about ways to improve practice. What we can say is that advocates of family literacy at the local, state, and national levels need not feel defensive about the foundation of family literacy, in concept or in practice. Research exists to suggest strongly that the basic concept and the early practice of family literacy programs are sound. Extensive anecdotal evidence also testifies to the effectiveness of family literacy programs. While we cannot yet quantify the results of family literacy, the research indicates that it is a solid approach to seemingly intractable problems of poverty and low literacy.

The family literacy movement needs to develop, fund, and execute a practical research agenda that will answer many of the unresolved questions about family literacy and its relationship to breaking the cycle of poverty and dependency. Policymakers need to know more about how the elements of family literacy work together and whether family literacy programs are cost effective. In addition, providers of family literacy services want to know more about how family literacy might be applied to different types of families and how their programs might be improved.

Elsewhere in this book, we will discuss a more complete research agenda for the family literacy movement. While there is much to be learned, we can take heart that the research and evaluations lead us to two simple conclusions:

- **Family literacy programs improve the lives of all participants — parents, children, and families.**

- **Family literacy programs help to break the intergenerational cycle of poverty and dependency.**

These research results should be enough to encourage policymakers and citizens alike to find out how to provide family literacy to every community that needs it in America. In the next chapters, we will discuss exactly that — how to start and operate effective family literacy programs and what should be done at the state level to encourage their creation.

ENDNOTES

[1] John Berreuta-Clement, Lawrence Schweinhart, Stephen Barnett, Ann Epstein, & David Weikart, *Changed Lives: The Effects of the Perry Preschool Program on Youths Through Age 19* (Ypsilanti: High/Scope Educational Research Foundation, 1984). The discussion on the High/Scope Perry Preschool Project was drawn, in large part, from this report.

[2] Ibid., 101.

[3] Ibid., 102.

[4] Judith A. Alamprese, "Strengthening the Knowledge Base in Adult Literacy: The Research Imperative," in Forrest P. Chisman and Associates, *Leadership for Literacy* (Washington: Jossey-Bass Publishers, 1990), 96–121; Jack Brizius & Susan Foster, *Enhancing Adult Literacy* (Washington: Council of State Policy and Planning Agencies, 1987), Chapter 5.

[5] Heather Weiss, Speech at National Conference on Family Literacy (Louisville: National Center for Family Literacy, April 1992).

[6] U.S. Department of Education, *National Evaluation of the Even Start Family Literacy Program, Executive Summary* (Washington: U.S. Department of Education, October 28, 1991), 2.

[7] National Center for Family Literacy, "Toyota Families for Learning Program, Data Summary" (Louisville: National Center for Family Literacy, January 20, 1992); National Center for Family Literacy, "National Center for Family Literacy Follow-up Studies, 1988–1990, The Children" (Louisville: National Center for Family Literacy, January 1991); Robert J. Popp, "Summary of Research for the Kenan Trust Model Family Literacy Programs" (Louisville: National Center for Family Literacy, July 3, 1991); Don Seaman, Robert J. Popp, "Follow-up Study of the Impact of the Kenan Model for Family Literacy" (Louisville: National Center for Family Literacy, Spring 1991); National Center for Family Literacy, "Model Sites Follow-up Study" (Louisville: National Center for Family Literacy, June 25, 1991); Robert J. Popp, "Past and Present Educational Experiences of Parents Who Enrolled in Kenan Trust Family Literacy Programs" (Louisville: National Center for Family Literacy, November 20, 1991).

[8] Don Seamon, *op cit.*, p. 29.

[9] National Center for Family Literacy, "Toyota Families for Learning Program, Data Summary" (Louisville: National Center for Family Literacy, January 20, 1992).

[10] National Center for Family Literacy, "National Center for Family Literacy Follow-up Studies, 1988–1990, The Children" (Louisville: National Center for Family Literacy, January 1991).

[11] National Center for Family Literacy, "Family Literacy Program Shows Promise in Raising Literacy Levels in America's At-Risk Families, Press Release" (Louisville: National Center for Family Literacy, August 15, 1991).

[12] National Center for Family Literacy, "What Parents Say About Participation in Family Literacy Programs" (Louisville: National Center for Family Literacy, June 25, 1991).

Chapter 5

BUILDING A COMMUNITY FAMILY LITERACY PROGRAM

Although the family literacy movement is growing by leaps and bounds, the chances are that your community does not offer a family literacy program. In fact, your primary motive in obtaining this book may be to find out how to start a family literacy program in your own community.

This chapter is designed to serve as your informal adviser as you consider whether to undertake the challenge of beginning a community family literacy program. It is aimed at a single individual or small group of people who are interested in family literacy, but its lessons could also be used by an energized businessperson, a local elected official, a statewide policymaker, or a foundation executive who wants to try to bring family literacy to a specific community.

While this chapter provides a step-by-step summary of how to develop a family literacy program, it is only a starting point. Organizations such as the National Center for Family Literacy, the Barbara Bush Foundation for

Family Literacy, the Business Council for Effective Literacy, or other organizations listed at the end of this book can also help with more specific questions about how to build a community family literacy program.

FIVE STEPS FOR FAMILY LITERACY IN YOUR COMMUNITY

Although there are hundreds of family literacy programs now operating all across America, no two are exactly alike. Each family literacy program must be tailored to the community it serves. Yet all of these programs share a common ancestry, and program providers have had similar experiences in getting their programs started. The process of developing a successful family literacy program may be summarized in five steps:

- Prepare your community for family literacy.
- Tailor a model program to suit your community's needs.
- Obtain institutional support.
- Raise the resources to do a good job.
- Implement and evaluate your program.

These five steps encompass a myriad of tasks that you will have to accomplish to get a family literacy program or programs operating in your community. Do not be daunted by their complexity or difficulty. Many others — parents, educators, librarians, businesspeople — have started family literacy programs successfully, and there are resources available to help you do the same. Those who have started family literacy programs advise: don't try to do it alone. You will find that many tasks can be shared and the experience of starting a family literacy program in your community will be an especially rewarding one.

PREPARE YOUR COMMUNITY FOR FAMILY LITERACY

As you begin a family literacy program in your community, how you accomplish your goal will depend, in part, on what role you now play in the life of the community. If you work in the school system, as a policy-maker or as an employee, your tactics in preparing your community for family literacy will be slightly different than if you are an elected leader or a concerned citizen. Nevertheless, to get a family literacy program started, you will have to accomplish a number of tasks related to preparing your community to support family literacy. (See sidebar on p. 79 for program prototype.)

GET A COLLABORATIVE GROUP TOGETHER
Based on your knowledge of the need for and benefits of family literacy, select a small steering or work group to help you in the task of preparing your community for family literacy. Include members of the major institutions and agencies you will be working with, especially the schools, social service agencies, and advocacy groups for adult literacy. You will also want to include representatives from the business community and concerned parents. You will need the support of a group. You cannot hope to start a program alone.

If you are the mayor or a local elected official, of course, it will be easier to convene a working group. If not, be sure to include an elected official at this point. Local officials can develop a collaborative approach among local public and nonprofit agencies, including educational institutions. At some point, each community will require that a collaborative team be developed. A sponsoring agency or individual can be responsible for convening and organizing the collaborative team.

There are other institutions in the community that could be helpful to your program. Job training programs, welfare and other social service agencies, other child care providers, vocational training programs, and community college programs can all be vital links the participating parents need. Getting these organizations involved while the program is still in the development stages can assure their commitment to participation and program success.

When the collaborative group convenes, it might want to use videotapes available from the National Center for Family Literacy, the Barbara Bush Foundation for Family Literacy, or summaries of the experience in cities participating in the Toyota Families for Learning program. All of these examples show the broad range of collaborative partners, funding sources, and the diversity of the lead agencies. To see how communities have organized themselves to address this issue, the group may also want to review the experience of Mesa, Arizona; Richmond, Virginia; New Orleans, Louisiana; and Fort Lauderdale, Florida. The National Center for Family Literacy can provide information about contacts in these cities.

DEFINE YOUR COMMUNITY AND THE PEOPLE YOU PLAN TO SERVE

The first task for the working group should be to define the community or group of people that should be served. Is the community defined by the boundaries of the school district? Perhaps you are dealing with family literacy issues in a rural county that spans several school districts. Or are you really trying to serve only a few blocks in a densely populated city? A community need not be defined solely by geography. Do you envision a family literacy program that encompasses parents and children from a range of income groups? Are you focusing attention on mothers who are at home with their children, on working parents with small children, or on employees and their families?

As you define the community or group of people you plan to serve, it will be important to be sensitive to the cultural diversity of the community. Since family literacy is aimed at strengthening families, you will need to be familiar with the culture in which these families are rooted.

A collaborative planning group also needs to be as clear as possible about the "customers" to be served through a community family literacy program. The working group needs to attend to this issue for two reasons. First, you need to plan a program that will be tailored to the needs of parents and children in the community you are planning to serve. The program will be quite different if you are serving working mothers and children, for example, than if you are trying to attract mothers who are staying home with small children. Second, how you define the community you are trying to serve will affect your ability to attract certain kinds of financing.

ESTIMATE HOW MANY PEOPLE CAN BENEFIT FROM THE PROGRAM

If you are a policymaker pulling together agencies and concerned citizens to address the issues of undereducation in your community, you already know how important it is to get a good needs assessment under way. Whether you are a private citizen or a public official, when you start to build your case for family literacy, you will want to estimate the size of the group to be served as clearly and accurately as possible. Often, a school district or the service area of a local school will be the appropriate level of analysis. In a large city, the community or target group may live in a small geographical area or share characteristics, such as being mothers on welfare or working in a single place.

Toyota Families for Learning Program Prototype for Building a Community Family Literacy Program

The focus of the Toyota Families for Learning Program (TFLP) is on collaboration among local agencies in the design, implementation, and evaluation stages. Each city participating in the program offers an individual approach to collaboration, reflecting the business personality of the sponsoring agency, yet each proceeds through the same elements of a team-building process:

PREPARE YOUR COMMUNITY FOR FAMILY LITERACY

The first goal of the TFLP program is to develop models of collaboration and co-ordination that allow cities to utilize existing resources to implement family literacy programs.

TAILOR A MODEL PROGRAM TO SUIT YOUR COMMUNITY'S NEEDS

The model to be used in the TFLP was developed as a comprehensive approach to break the intergenerational cycle of illiteracy and undereducation. It is based on the highly successful PACE program in Kentucky and the Kenan Trust Family Literacy Model. Each city builds collaborative partners to implement the model. In some cases, both home-based and center-based services are provided. In some, volunteers participate. The way in which the model is implemented depends on the needs and resources of each community.

OBTAIN INSTITUTIONAL SUPPORT

Each city is required to provide a sponsoring agency. This agency is responsible for providing the leadership to connect the program's collaborative partners who bring a variety of valuable resources and linkages to the projects. One criteria for selecting grant recipients is the documented commitment of the key officials in government and education.

RAISE THE RESOURCES TO DO A GOOD JOB

The Toyota project provides each selected city $225,000 in grant funds but each program must secure additional funding to support this comprehensive program. These funds are obtained from a variety of state and community resources including the traditional federal and state programs as well as funds from banks, housing authorities, urban leagues, universities, local governments, junior leagues, libraries, foundations, and many others.

IMPLEMENT AND EVALUATE YOUR PROGRAM

A collaborative team is set up in each city to assure effective implementation. Each TFLP participant is required to participate in an assessment and evaluation, with many of the data collection forms and some of the evaluation instruments provided by NCFL.

Source: National Center for Family Literacy

A needs analysis should be based on a combination of good statistics and community knowledge. Here is one way to complete a mini-needs assessment. First, find out from your school system how many children in your community take advantage of the free and reduced price lunch program. A good proxy for the percentage of low-income parents is the percentage of free and reduced price lunch participants in any school or school district. The percentage of free lunch participants is the rock-bottom percentage for the very poor in your community.

Second, get an estimate of the number or percentage of adults in your community with low literacy skills. Except in a few extraordinarily fortunate communities, this is likely to be above 15 percent and may be much more. Find out the number of adults lacking high school credentials and the current dropout rate. If you have an adult literacy coalition or are part of one, see if they have any estimates concerning the need. Your local job training program, welfare office, or business-education coalition may also have some estimates you can rely on. Be sure you find out how they arrived at their estimates.

Third, find out how many families with children under the age of five are in your community. These data are readily available from the Census Bureau, your state data center, or from your town planning office. You can also estimate from the number of kindergarten children in your area how many families have prekindergarten children.

Finally, apply both the low-income and adult literacy need percentages to the number of families with children under five. This should give you a range of numbers equal to the number of families who could be helped by family literacy programs. If the numbers are larger than about 75–100, there are enough families to start a family literacy program.

Even if this needs analysis will result in a number far higher than this, you should do the exercise. As a policymaker or a concerned citizen, you will need to be able to show others the extent of the demand for family literacy and where the appropriate agencies should target their efforts. These numbers will also be needed when resources are allocated to provide budget justifications.

ASSESS THE COMMUNITY'S HUMAN RESOURCES

To implement a family literacy program, a substantial reservoir of community leadership must be tapped. If the collaborative effort has been started by policymakers, agencies will have to make sure that they assign their best people to organizing and implementing family literacy programs. If the sponsoring group is new, members will need to scan the community, the schools, and business and industry for persons who will understand the value of family literacy and who have the imagination and energy to bring a start-up program to life. These skills are usually in short supply, and organizers need to reach out for leaders early in the development process.

While a great deal of training and technical assistance is available through the National Center for Family Literacy and others, you will still need talented "public entrepreneurs" to get a top-quality program under way. Experience with the Toyota Families for Learning project and elsewhere has shown that talented people are enthusiastic about working in family literacy efforts if the sponsoring group shows strong support.

EXAMINE THE POSSIBILITIES FOR FUNDING

Any collaborative effort to start a family literacy program will have to make a reconnaissance of the available resources in the community. These can range from small amounts available through the local schools to larger state programs or the federal Even Start and Head Start programs. A number of foundations and private companies are also funding local family literacy programs.

For some help in identifying funding sources, you may wish to order a publication of the National Center for Family Literacy: *A Guide to Funding Sources for Family Literacy*. This publication will help you find out which federal, state, local, and private sector funding options might best suit your community. In addition, Project Literacy U.S. (PLUS) has produced an excellent videotape on fund raising for literacy programs.

While it is not necessary to identify all your funding at this stage, it will be helpful to assess your community's assets since it is highly likely that funding your family literacy program will require a variety of sources. You may be surprised where financial support may be found, among businesses, community foundations, libraries, churches, and civic groups. It is also important at this stage to develop a clear rationale for funding a family literacy program instead of other services or programs.

TAILOR A PROGRAM TO SUIT YOUR COMMUNITY'S NEEDS

One of the advantages of starting a family literacy program today is that other communities have begun successful programs in cities and towns all over the country. Because of the unique history of family literacy, a number of models using the four components have been developed and "field-tested" by pioneers in the field. Many mistakes have been made and corrected, so you need not make them. Recruitment strategies, curricula, and staffing patterns have been tested and fine-tuned, so that you can learn what seems to work the best.

When you are designing a family literacy program for your community, we strongly advise you to learn all you can about one or more of the successful models and then customize that program to meet the needs of your community. Because of the work you did at the beginning of the process, you already have much of the information you will need to choose a good model and tailor it to your own needs. Be sure training is available and that you are connected to an organization that will support you. Although a program has been successful, it may not be replicable if no training exists.

Three different models of family literacy programs are described next and summarized in the chart on pages 84–85. Many other models exist. For example, some family literacy programs that offer all four components have joined forces with volunteer organizations such as Literacy Volunteers of America (LVA) or Vista, or with libraries or Chapter I programs. Also, a family literacy program in Eau Clair, Wisconsin, is a comprehensive group-based model located at the YMCA and associated with Literacy Volunteers of America. The National Center for Family Literacy's project with the Bureau of Indian Affairs is a combination group-based/home-based program. The models presented here have been selected to illustrate the range of approaches family literacy providers may consider in tailoring programs to the needs of local communities.

THE GROUP-BASED MODEL

Perhaps the most extensive information and training are available on the group-based model family literacy programs. Many group-based programs developed with the assistance of the National Center for Family Literacy. The model described in the chart on pages 84–85 is probably the

most intensive type of program and embodies the four elements of family literacy discussed in Chapter 2. This model is one that has been replicated in almost every state, but may look very different in each location as its flexibility allows differing configurations of the four elements. The four-components concept is commonly referred to as the Kenan Model in honor of the original funders of the program.

Parents help their children learn in the preschool classroom, and they discover how to make learning fun at home as well.

The group-based model brings together parents or other adult caregivers with three- or four-year-old children for three days each week. Programs are usually located in elementary schools, but if a school site is not available the program may choose another location while maintaining a link with the school system. The group-based model stresses the school linkage because an important part of family literacy is to involve parents in the continuing education of their children.

The children participate in a high-quality preschool program while the adults learn skills in various academic areas. In addition, vocational

TAILORING FAMILY LITERACY PROGRAMS TO THE NEEDS OF LOCAL COMMUNITIES

FAMILY LITERACY MUST...

Be designed for parents in need of literacy skills and their children in need of a positive start to lifelong learning.

Provide quality education services based on sound adult instructional principles and developmentally appropriate practices in early childhood.

Provide services that are strongly connected through integration of the parts.

Involve intensity and duration.

Build upon family strengths.

Be provided by qualified staff with the skills and expertise to implement a comprehensive, quality program.

HOME-BASED PROGRAM

Child is given activity to complete with minimal help while parent and staff then work together on adult basic education/literacy skills.

Parental concerns are discussed and action plans developed jointly for dealing with critical issues such as parenting and employment.

Parents and staff work with child on jointly planned activities to enhance learning.

Home visit is concluded with joint planning for follow-up activities and preparation for next visit.

Home visitor(s) arrive at family's home.

Child chooses activity and has opportunity to play with parent.

COMBINATION OF GROUP-BASED AND HOME-BASED PROGRAM

Families receive at least two home visits per month.

Parents and children attend group-based program a minimum of twice per month.

Parents are involved in group instruction in adult basic education/literacy or participate in parent support groups while children attend preschool.

During home visits, skills and concepts from all areas are reinforced, and attention is paid to facilitating lifelong learning in the home environment.

Parents and children are brought together for positive parent-child interaction through a play experience.

Group time is concluded with an activity for all families, which promotes transfer to home.

Parents and children arrive at school together.

GROUP-BASED PROGRAM

Parents and children are brought together for parent-child interaction through play.

All parents and children are brought together after this play experience for an activity to promote transfer to home.

Parents are involved in a parent group where they receive support, information, referrals, and develop problem-solving skills for dealing with critical issues in their lives.

Parents attend adult basic education classes while children attend preschool.

preparation is provided for adults through career counseling, student assessment, and instruction to develop employability skills. This component of the model is designed to establish a pathway for adults from literacy instruction to work or further schooling.

The group-based model programs also include specific times when parents and children work and play together during the school day. Parents help their children learn in the preschool classroom, and they discover how to make learning fun at home. Parents are asked to apply effective parenting strategies with their own children as they learn them in the parent-education portion of the program.

The staff. Because it seeks to provide a high-quality experience in all four elements of family literacy, the group-based model requires relatively extensive staffing. The professional staff includes at least one early childhood teacher, one early childhood assistant, and one adult education teacher in addition to the program administrator. Larger programs are built on multiples of this staffing pattern, often with part-time professionals fulfilling more specialized roles. Volunteers may be used as well as paid staff.

Qualifications for staff in the group-based model are also relatively high, but often experience can be substituted for academic education. Early childhood educators, for example, should possess a bachelor's degree and certification by the state to teach early childhood education or an associate degree and two years successful experience in early childhood teaching. The early childhood assistant should have a high school degree and two years experience. Adult educators must have similar credentials with more experience, since program designers believe that experience with adult learners in the community is very important to maintaining motivation among parents.

The most important part of staffing the group-based model is making sure that staff believe in and practice teamwork. Designers stress that "although staff members have distinct roles in the program, they must function as a team."[1] Teamwork is crucial because a good family literacy program requires that staff members be flexible in their roles. Adult educators will have to teach pre-employment skills and provide job counseling and work with early childhood teachers to facilitate parent support groups and help develop parenting skills. All staff members are required to interact with parents and children, as well as participate in planning activities. When you are tailoring the group-based model to your own needs, you should be especially aware of the need to recruit high-quality staff who can be part of a team.

The preschool curriculum. Both the adult education and preschool curriculum in the group-based model are designed to be state of the art. Group-based model designers recommend that the High/Scope Preschool Curriculum or a similar developmental preschool curriculum be used. Training in this curriculum may be obtained through the National Center for Family Literacy. The High/Scope Curriculum stresses "that children are active learners who learn best from activities they plan and carry out themselves. Children in this program have control over what happens to them. The emphasis on planning, working, and evaluating establishes personal responsibility in the child."[2]

When working with economically deprived children, it is especially important that the curriculum allow children opportunities to explore, investigate, and inquire. As a result, the preschool curriculum is not rigid but allows children to construct their own knowledge, initiate learning, make choices and decisions, and learn through experience. As the National Center for Family Literacy manual for administrators states:

> One thing we do know about undereducated, economically deprived families is that the idea of their being able to control their own lives is very often a dream. By starting the children in an environment of shared control and by involving the parents from the beginning, we are creating a climate where they can take risks and feel safe trying new learning and parenting strategies. Children learn by doing! Qualified teachers and parents must support the doing![3]

The preschool curriculum recommended in the group-based model is emphatically not a direct instruction model. Rather, it is an open framework curriculum that consists of a prepared physical environment, supportive teaching strategies, a consistent daily routine, guiding key experience statements, and a child development assessment system built on teacher observation. Since the basic philosophy is built on the belief that children construct their own knowledge, the curriculum provides instruction through playful experiences.

The approach to adult education. In the adult education arena, the group-based model emphasizes that for adult participants, literacy instruction and adult education must be customized to the needs of each adult learner. These needs vary with the individual. Some adults will seek help in preparing for employment. Others may need to prepare for the GED test or acquire basic skills leading to job training. With the use of informal assessments, instruction can begin immediately. A formal assessment is completed after the student has been prepared "to test."

By tailoring a program to the adult's needs, the role of the teacher in family literacy programs changes from instructor to facilitator. The program designers suggest that "Collaboration between student and student as well as between instructor and student emphasizes the theory that instructors of adults should serve more as facilitators who help adults discover what they already know than as teachers who hold the key and the lock on knowledge."[4] Adult learning becomes more of a joint exploration than a passive experience where the teacher teaches and the adult student learns.

The subject matter of the curriculum focuses on reading and language development, mathematics, communication skills, job readiness, and self-awareness. It also stresses higher order thinking skills or critical thinking. Ideally, these skills will be acquired in the functional context of life for the adult learner. This means, for example, that parents learn to read better by using reading to solve problems they face at home or at work. They also learn to use materials that will help them assist their children in learning. The adult literacy curriculum attempts to build on the strong motivation parents have to improve themselves so they can get a better job or help their children in school.

A key part of the group-based model curriculum is an emphasis on evaluation of the adult learner's progress. The program assesses where adults stand in terms of the proficiencies they will need to improve daily life, get a job, or pass the GED examination. Program designers stress the need to give feedback to adult learners about their progress as often as possible in the learning process.

The final part of the group-based adult curriculum involves acquiring

specific skills aimed at getting and holding a job. Family literacy practitioners have found that the goals of most adults include improving their economic circumstances as well as helping their children. Pre-employment instruction gives adults the basic skills they need to apply for and get a job, to seek further education, and to manage money. When added to the basic skills adults learn through the program, this package of pre-employment skills equips them to "take the next step" on the road to economic independence and a more stable family life.

Adult learners acquire basic skills through working with materials that come from the context of their lives. The lesson pictured here revolves around the information found on food labels.

Parent support and time together. In the group-based model there are two critical parts of family literacy: one brings parents together to support one another; and the other provides an opportunity for children and parents to work together. Model designers say that these two components are absolutely crucial to the success of the program and should be included as regular parts of the daily schedule.

During the time when parents and children are together, parents provide support for their children at play. This seemingly simple activity is fraught with meaning, especially for young and undereducated parents who have little time to play with their children at home. This time involves all the parents and their children in activities that stimulate and reinforce interaction within the family. Children choose what they would like to do and the parents support their efforts by asking questions, entering the play, and adding more materials or ideas as they see fit. As the Kenan program developers report, "the parents learn that 'play is the child's work' and that parents need to support their preschooler's play. This time is designed so that parents can practice the art of supporting their children in a risk-free environment."[5]

Just as parents and children need time to learn how to learn together, parents need time to discuss what parenting is all about and to help each other overcome obstacles and solve problems. In the group-based model, a specific time is scheduled for this parent support activity. During this time, parents generate topics of discussion that relate to parenting and other critical life issues. These include budgeting, health and nutrition, stress management, and relationship problems. This time also serves to bring staff into close contact with the parents so they can identify needs and interests and make appropriate referrals to community services. In addition, the support of their peers enables parents to share experiences and learn group process skills and problem-solving techniques. The support group also serves as a vehicle through which parents build self-worth and self-confidence.

Training. Developers of the group-based model family literacy programs believe that continuous training and professional development for the staff are a key to success in family literacy. Implementation assistance and training in the group-based model is provided by the National Center for Family Literacy, and many of the program operators credit their initial success in large part to the intensive training they received. If you decide to use the group-based model in your own community, you should be sure to budget enough money for initial and follow-up training.

How to find out more about the group-based model. Detailed information about the group-based model is available from the National Center for Family Literacy in Louisville, Kentucky. After July 1, 1993, the address will be National Center for Family Literacy, Waterfront Plaza, 325 W. Main Street, Louisville, Kentucky 40202, (502) 584-1133. The Center is also working with home-based and combination models and can provide comprehensive training and implementation assistance for most variations of family literacy programs.

In addition, the group-based model programs welcome visitors who are interested in developing similar programs. Visits can also be arranged to home-based or combination models through the National Center for Family Literacy or by calling or writing program directors identified by the Center. The Center also conducts policy seminars for policymakers who are considering family literacy and want to explore the available models.

THE HOME-BASED MODEL

Many communities have chosen to implement home-based family literacy programs as their primary mode of service delivery or in combination with a group-based approach. Home-based programs are both popular and effective for several reasons.

A primary reason for providing home-based services is to reach families who might not otherwise have access to these services, such as families living in isolated rural areas or those lacking transportation. Families who might otherwise avoid formal service providers because of negative experiences or a lack of trust in the "helping profession" can also benefit from home-based services before transitioning them into a group-based program. A home-based service delivery model is also very effective with mothers who are pregnant or have infants. This approach also provides more flexibility for programs in scheduling and for programs that have inadequate space available for center services. Finally, many Head Start and family-focused "Birth-to-Three"programs have very successfully implemented home-based programs that lend themselves to adaptations to include the four elements of a quality family literacy program. Even Start legislation provides funds for home-based family literacy services.

The staff configuration of a home-based approach depends greatly on the program design. For programs that are primarily home-based, staff qualifications must include extensive experience in family-focused service delivery, a solid understanding of empowerment strategies, and comprehensive knowledge in all four components of family literacy. Some programs have chosen to send an adult educator and an early childhood educator out on home visits together; other programs, which have staff with experience in both areas, provide home-based services alone, with support from other professionals. Others yet have provided the early childhood, intergenerational, and parent-time components in the home and have coordinated with another service provider to provide the adult education in the home or at a center or school.

There are many similarities between the group-based and home-based approaches. Both incorporate and integrate all four components, provide quality educational services based on sound instructional principles, and build upon family strengths. The difference is mainly where these services take place.

In one home-based model, each family receives a minimum of one home visit per week, which lasts between one-and-a-half to two hours. During this time parents and children have an opportunity for positive interactions with the support of the home visitor(s). Parents and staff work with the child on jointly planned activities to enhance learning. This parallels the early childhood component of the group-based approach. Next, the child chooses an activity and has an opportunity to play with the parent. Following the parent-child interaction, the child is given a task to complete independently or with minimal assistance. At that time the parent and staff work on the parent's issues and goals related to adult basic education, parenting, employment, and other critical life issues. The home visit is concluded with joint planning by parent and staff for the following week's visit, and a plan for following through on what was covered on that day's visit is developed. Parents who are in need of additional adult basic skills beyond the individual study on the home visit are assigned a tutor. As you can see, all four components are included and the parent is actively involved in the entire home visit.

THE COMBINATION MODEL

In a combination program the parents and children attend a group-based program a minimum of twice per month. During this time the parents may be involved in group instruction in adult basic education/literacy and/or attend parent groups while their children are in an early childhood program. Parents and children are brought together to increase positive parent-child interactions through play and to provide parents an opportunity to better understand how to facilitate their children's learning. The group experience concludes with an activity to reinforce skills through transfer to home.

During the home visits, skills and concepts from all areas are reinforced and individual attention is paid to facilitating lifelong learning within the home environment. If the home-based services are supplemental in nature to the center experience, then the existing center staff can be utilized for the home visits. Many programs assign existing staff to individual families based on primary areas of need. For example, if a parent is most in need of reinforcement of adult education, the adult educator would provide services to that family. If this is not possible because of staffing patterns or contract limitations, then the home visitor is responsible for collaborating closely with the adult educator to ensure appropriate reinforcement of skills in the primary area of need. Once again, the team must work very closely together for quality programming that focuses on the *family* as a whole as opposed to the individual family members in a fragmented approach.

The components of adult education, early childhood, parent-child interaction, and parent group can be achieved on home visits successfully. However, it is the recommendation of the National Center for Family Literacy that the parents be provided some opportunity to benefit from group instruction in adult education. In an effort to promote a network of supportive peers it's also recommended that parents be brought together periodically in a group setting. Most family literacy programs also encourage parents to volunteer in the schools on a regular basis and to be actively involved in the education of their child(ren). This often affords parents the chance to work with groups such as parent-teacher organizations. Certainly children benefit greatly from group experiences as well; therefore it is suggested that at the very least occasional group socialization opportunities are provided for the children enrolled in family literacy programs.

WORKPLACE-BASED MODEL

A new concept in family literacy is linking the group-based model to the workplace. While there are programs in operation that attempt to link workplace-based adult literacy to the home and to extend the benefits of literacy instruction to children, no model is currently in operation of a family literacy workplace-based model.

The concept of the workplace-based model is that a family literacy program would be housed in the workplace. The parent would be employed at the site and the workplace would operate a full-day child care program. The workplace would release the parent for time to interact with the children and to participate in adult literacy instruction.

The instruction would be tied directly to the requirements of the workplace, but the family literacy program would help participants generalize the skills they learn and apply them to their home situation, to their relationship with their children, and to their relationship with the schools.

The staff would be essentially the same as in the group-based model, but the adult literacy instructors would be trained in workplace literacy instruction. Staff would concentrate on employment needs, GED needs, and parenting skill needs of the parent. Skills that are generic to each of these areas would become the core competencies of the workplace-based model. All skills learned in the workplace would be tied back to the family to the extent possible.

A large hotel chain in Hawaii has expressed interest in this concept as it would help to reduce the large turnover of employees in the hotel industry and provide a positive influence on the next generation. As our economy is faced with fewer workers, greater demands on employees, and a greater number of non–English-speaking employees, the application of this concept should catch on.

OBTAIN INSTITUTIONAL SUPPORT

After you have chosen a model for your program or combined the elements of a family literacy program into a model tailored to your community, you must begin to solidify the support of community leaders and their institutions.

Perhaps the most important institution to the family literacy program's success is the school. Whether center-based, home-based, or workplace-based, the school's involvement is essential. Family literacy programs are designed to increase the comfort of parents in their children's schools, better prepare children for the school experience, and involve parents as helpers in the schools. The collaborative sponsoring group should work closely with school personnel, securing their participation in the design of the program to be sure that they are committed to the goals of family literacy and to the program's success.

To avoid misunderstandings that may stand in the way of program integration, it is important to involve all appropriate community agencies in the early planning. Otherwise, social service and child care providers may feel threatened by a new family literacy program. Adult literacy providers may feel that literacy is within their purview and be reluctant to cooperate with a new family literacy effort.

Relationships with each of these organizations must be negotiated so the best resources of each are brought together to build your family literacy program. The best way to negotiate these relationships is to involve these agencies in the collaborative planning group from the beginning. The Toyota Families for Learning program experiences have taught that creating such collaborative groups is the best way to succeed.

Family literacy providers stress the importance of integration of services at the local level. This, they feel, is a major key to the eventual success of a family literacy program. The focus of family literacy is on the family, while the focus of many social, health, welfare, and job training services is usually on a problem or on the individual. Cross training — simultaneously training program staff from all participating agencies — has proved to be a valuable tool in building a team of professionals who are dedicated to the goals of the family literacy program and are willing to bring the resources of their own agencies to bear on furthering the goals of participating families.

RAISE THE RESOURCES FOR EXCELLENCE

A major problem faced by a prospective family literacy provider is where to find the funds to support the program. Fortunately, many others have gone before and have identified a variety of funding sources; however, it will still require a significant amount of work to apply for the funds and, if necessary, piece together funds from different sources.

The major sources of public funds for family literacy *per se* are Even Start, Head Start, Chapter I of the Federal Education Consolidation and

Improvement Act (compensatory education), Chapter II of the Federal Education Consolidation and Improvement Act (school improvement), and the Title XX Social Services Block Grants of the Social Security Act.[6]

Funds to support the adult literacy component include the Family Support Act, the Adult Education Act, the National Literacy Act, the Job Training Partnership Act, the VISTA program, the Bilingual Education Act, and the Carl Perkins Vocational Education Act. There are also many other public programs that can be used to support portions of the family literacy program. These include: the Wagner Peyser Discretionary Program 7(b); the Targeted Jobs Tax Credit, Library Services and Construction Act (Titles I and VI); and Community Services Block Grants. The sidebar on page 97 describes the funding sources for family literacy programs.

Private sector grants to support family literacy are also available from foundations and corporations. A major foundation that offers support is the Barbara Bush Foundation for Family Literacy.[7] There are thousands of grant-making foundations in the United States. Information about these foundations can be obtained through the Foundation Center[8] located in New York or in the reference section of your local public or college library. Cooperative public awareness programs with businesses in your community can help raise funds as well.

There are also many corporations in the United States that make contributions to education and literacy. Information about current corporate giving can be obtained through several sources:

- *The Directory of Corporate Philanthropy*[9] — describes funding provided by the top 500 U.S. corporations.

- *Corporate Foundation Profiles*[10] — provides detailed information about the 234 largest corporate givers as well as descriptions of 701 corporations whose foundations provide major sources of funding.

- *The Taft Corporate Giving Directory*[11] — tracks corporations who are major funders of grants.

- *Make It Your Business: A Corporate Fundraising Guide for Literacy Programs*[12] — provides an introduction to the corporate giving environment and guidelines to raising corporate funds for literacy programs.

Funding Sources for Family Literacy

The National Literacy Act: The purpose of the act is to aid government agencies in setting goals, conducting literacy research, distributing research findings, and funding literacy programs. Among other provisions, the act funds state literacy resource centers, which help coordinate literacy services, provide training and technical assistance to instructors, and help literacy programs reach their targeted individuals.

The Adult Education Act: Under this legislation, funds are provided to states on a matching grant basis for the development of adult education for those who are sixteen and over and have not graduated from high school.

The Job Training Partnership Act: Providing remedial education to prepare adults to enter the labor force is an allowable activity under this act. Programs under this act that could be used include: Title IIA—disadvantaged youth and adults, Title IIB—summer youth employment; Title III—economic dislocation and worker adjustment assistance; the governor's 8 percent discretionary fund; and state education coordination grants. Title IIA and IIB funds flow through the local private industry councils and other funds can be accessed through the state job training agency.

The Elementary and Secondary Education Act: Programs under this act that could support family literacy include: Chapter 1—compensatory education, Even Start, and Chapter 2—school improvement. These funds flow through local education agencies.

Head Start: This is a direct grant program from the U.S. Department of Health and Human Services. Collaborative efforts with other agencies have become an important focus of Head Start. All Head Start programs are encouraged to have family literacy components by the end of 1992.

The Family Support Act: This act requires that Aid to Families with Dependent Children recipients participate in a jobs program or, if non–high-school, then an education program. The JOBS program makes provisions for high school or equivalency training, remedial education, and education for limited English proficiency. Family literacy services can be funded under this program. Funding questions should be directed to the state social service/welfare agency.

Other: The Title XX Social Service Block grant program, the Education of the Handicapped and the Rehabilitation Act, can also be used to support some of the costs of family literacy programs, as can a range of other federal programs. A complete list of funding sources can be found in the source document cited below.

Source: The National Center for Family Literacy, "A Guide to Funding Sources for Family Literacy," November 11, 1991

Your task will be to examine the array of funding sources, target those most promising given the particular model you have chosen, and prepare applications for funding. (Check your local public or college library for any of these sources.) You should thoroughly investigate public funding before contacting private sources. A good place to start is your state agency responsible for adult education. They can tell you what state and federal funds are available for adult literacy and they can direct you to contacts in other state agencies responsible for early childhood programs, training and vocational education, and community services.

You will probably have to combine several different funding sources in order to support your program. If you need help or examples of how to combine funding sources, contact the National Center for Family Literacy.[13] When you combine funding sources, you will have to pay attention to the grant cycles and how they relate to your program year.

Once you have selected the funding sources, you are ready to prepare the proposals. A good description of information to include in your proposal as well as a checklist for evaluating proposals is found in the National Center for Family Literacy's publication, *A Guide to Funding Sources for Family Literacy*.

In preparing your proposal, it will be to your advantage to stress local program integration to the extent possible, the focus on the family, the strong link with the school, and opportunities for advancement of adult learners that you have built into the program. For further assistance, contact the organizations listed in the sidebar on page 99.

IMPLEMENT AND EVALUATE YOUR PROGRAM

When you begin program implementation, it will be important to provide preservice training for your staff and for staff of cooperating agencies if possible. Training should stress the importance of program and staff evaluation.

Evaluation is important for several reasons. First, family literacy programs will have to describe the effectiveness of their efforts. They should be able to identify what difference the program has made in the lives of the participants and for the community. Second, they will have to clearly assess individual progress of the parent and child participants. Third, they should be able to assess the effectiveness of each component

Where to Find Help

National Center for Family Literacy—Has developed model programs, materials, and training programs to support family literacy programs.

> Until July 1, 1993, 401 South 4th Avenue, Suite 610, Louisville, KY 40202
> (502) 584-1133. After July 1, 1993, Waterfront Plaza, 325 W. Main St.,
> Louisville, KY 40202 (502) 584-1133.

Barbara Bush Foundation for Family Literacy—Has developed informational materials to support family reading programs.

> 1002 Wisconsin Ave. NW, Washington, DC 20007
> (202) 338-2006

Business Council for Effective Literacy—Provides information concerning literacy in the business community and workplace literacy.

> 1221 Avenue of the Americas, 35th floor,
> New York, NY 10020 (212) 512-2415/2412

National Coalition of Title 1/Chapter 1 Parents (National Parent Center)— Provides a voice for Chapter 1 parents at the federal, regional, state, and local level.

> Edmonds School Building, 9th and D Streets NE
> Washington, DC 20002 (202) 547-9286

National Committee for Citizens in Education—Has publications for parents and other family members who want to learn how to become more involved in their children's education.

> 10840 Little Patuxent Parkway, Suite 301, Columbia, NC 21044

Parent-Teacher Associations—National, state, and local PTAs have many resources and materials that can be used at home and at school to support children's learning.

> National PTA, Department D, 700 North Rush St.
> Chicago, IL 60611-2571, or contact your local PTA

Project PLUS—Has developed a tape of the discussion of four experts on the funding of literacy programs, with two experts from the public sector and two from the private sector.

> PBS Project PLUS, WQED, 4802 Fifth Ave.
> Pittsburgh, PA 15213 (412) 622-1320

Source: National Center for Family Literacy

and identify ways to improve the program so that it better serves the participants. Finally, they should be able to assess the skills of the staff and identify ways that skills can be improved.

Program implementation should be inextricably linked with evaluation. To quote Sharon Darling, "We must implement, then assess, then revise and reassess. This process must continue throughout the life of the program."

Building a family literacy program can be an exciting and creative process.[14] We know the essential components of effective family literacy programs and there are many models to choose from. Persons interested in starting programs should carefully judge the needs in their community and creatively design a program that will best meet these needs. Family literacy providers are artists, designers, managers, researchers, and evaluators. Their efforts will contribute to the advancement of the state of the art in family literacy.

ENDNOTES

[1] National Center for Family Literacy, "Administrator/Policy Maker Training Manual" (Louisville: National Center for Family Literacy, September 24, 1991).

[2] David Weikart in National Center for Family Literacy, "Administrator/Policy Maker Training Manual" (Louisville: National Center for Family Literacy, September 24, 1991).

[3] National Center for Family Literacy, "Administrator/Policy Maker Training Manual" (Louisville: National Center for Family Literacy, September 24, 1991).

[4] Ibid.

[5] Ibid.

[6] Ibid.

[7] Much of the information presented in this section is drawn from: National Center for Family Literacy, *A Guide to Funding Sources for Family Literacy* (Louisville: National Center for Family Literacy). To receive information about funding, contact: The Barbara Bush Foundation for Family Literacy, 1002 Wisconsin Avenue, NW, Washington, DC 20007 (202) 338-2006.

[8] To receive information about the resource guides published by the Foundation Center, contact: The Foundation Center, 79 Fifth Avenue, New York, NY (800) 424-9836.

[9] To receive this directory, contact: the Public Management Institute, 358 Brannan, San Francisco, CA 94107, (415) 896-1900.

[10] To receive this directory, contact: The Foundation Center, 79 Fifth Avenue, New York, NY 10003 (800) 424-9836.

[11] To receive this directory, contact: The Taft Group, 5130 Marathon Boulevard NW, Washington, DC (202) 966-7086.

[12] To receive this directory, contact: Business Council for Effective Literacy, 1221 Avenue of the Americas, 35th floor, New York, NY 10020, (212) 512-2415.

[13] For detailed instruction on funding sources and how to combine them see: National Center for Family Literacy, *A Guide to Funding Sources for Family Literacy* (Louisville: National Center for Family Literacy).

[14] For further information and a framework for family literacy program evaluation, contact the National Center for Family Literacy, Waterfront Plaza, 325 W. Main Street, Louisville, KY 40202, (502) 584-1133 and the Illinois Literacy Resource Development Center, 200 South Frederick, Rantoul, IL 61866, (217) 893-1318.

Chapter 6

DEVELOPING A STATE FAMILY LITERACY INITIATIVE

For the most part, family literacy has been growing person by person, community by community. In some states, however, political leaders and educators have embraced family literacy as an important facet of policies designed to strengthen families and promote economic growth through upgrading the literacy of adults.

In this chapter, we will discuss some of the key issues that family literacy advocates must address in order to promote and develop statewide family literacy efforts. In addition, we will address issues that state policymakers need to confront when considering the development of family literacy initiatives.

POLITICAL LEADERS: HOW DO THEY FEEL ABOUT FAMILY LITERACY?

Unlike many other movements, family literacy has a crucial advantage at the state level. Most governors and many state legislators possess positive impressions of the family literacy concept. Although no single governor has taken on

First Lady of Hawaii, Lynne Waihee, has nurtured the family literacy movement in her state from a seed of an idea to a successful program "in full bloom."

family literacy as a crusade, the consciousness of state leaders has been raised in a number of ways: a Ford Foundation award for the PACE program, repeated mention of family literacy at National Governors' Association meetings, the efforts of the First Lady of Hawaii, and other positive media attention.

Family literacy is appealing to political leaders because it is oriented toward the family and toward reducing dependency. It also resonates with political leaders who believe that education reform efforts will not succeed without significant improvements in family functioning. Finally, since nearly all state political leaders have pledged to improve their state's economy through enhancing the skills of the labor force, family literacy's implicit promise of better educated adult workers is attractive.

As a result of these factors, the chances are that political leaders in your state will be inclined positively toward family literacy. Rhetorically, family literacy may be an easy sell. When political leaders find out that family literacy is not cheap, however, the fiscal realities of state and local government may combine to crush the hope that a major family literacy initiative can be mounted at the state level. In addition, many political leaders still believe that literacy problems can be solved by volunteers or through community-based institutions such as public libraries. They find it hard to understand the need for a comprehensive approach like family literacy.

Family literacy advocates should take time to find out where their key leaders stand on the concept of family literacy. It will be a worthwhile exercise to solicit—formally or informally—the opinions of the governor, the legislative leadership, key legislators on education and appropriations committees, and key cabinet officials. In many cases, when asked, they will point to small demonstration or other family-literacy-related programs that are now operating.

BUILDING THE CONSTITUENCY FOR FAMILY LITERACY

Even if you are fortunate enough to have political leadership that is familiar with family literacy and feels basically positive toward the idea, you are still a long way from a statewide initiative. To take the next step, you will have to build a constituency for family literacy. Despite its intuitive appeal, family literacy will not have a built-in constituency at the state capital. Family literacy advocates build their constituency by drawing support from major interest groups and from communities that have positive experiences with family literacy. There are several steps that you should take to build a strong constituency for family literacy.

FIND SOME ALLIES

You will find among program providers and state agency personnel many people who will intuitively understand the usefulness of family literacy, because they work every day with programs that don't offer the full range of services provided by family literacy programs. These people can be part of a cadre of supporters in a state capital.

Another place to seek out allies for family literacy is among the professional organizations of teachers, social workers, and others who deal every day with the consequences of low literacy skills and the lack of parental involvement in education. Teachers should be supportive, because family literacy programs improve the readiness of students. Social workers, child welfare advocates, and others in the human services arena should also be natural allies. These groups will only become allies if the fiscal consequences of supporting family literacy are not detrimental to their main priorities, however.

Considerable sympathy and support can be gained within the business community for family literacy. Business support comes not only because family literacy is such a good idea, but also because business people are looking for programs that have high returns for relatively low investments. They seek the "double utility" as well as the common sense of improving opportunities for both parents and children alike.

PORTRAY FAMILY LITERACY IN THE CONTEXT OF KEY STATE PRIORITIES

Because family literacy involves welding together several strands of thought and action related to education, adult literacy, and even economic development policy, state policymakers have had some difficulty in imagining just where family literacy "fits in" within the program categories that have traditionally dominated thinking at the state level.

When you approach state leaders, you should be aware of the state policy landscape to see where family literacy might best fit into a statewide priority. If state leaders are concentrating on education reform, for example, it will be a good idea to stress the relationship of family literacy to school reform: family literacy helps to achieve two of the national education goals. Family literacy can "fit in" as a means to greater parental involvement in the school, as a prekindergarten program with a plus, or as a parent education program.

If economic development is the state priority, family literacy advocates can help build support of business and labor by talking about the motivation for adult learning inherent in family literacy. Many of those interested in economic development believe that motivating poor people to upgrade skills is a key part of work-force development. They understand that low-skilled adults will have a dual motivation to participate in family literacy programs: to help their children and to improve their skills.

In many states, governors and other political leaders are turning attention to the need to strengthen families. Family literacy brings families together for learning and helps adults become better parents. The parental

Wally Amos, President of the Uncle Nonamé Cookie Company, has championed the cause of literacy, lending his spirit to heighten public awareness. He is pictured here with Dr. Ben Currin, President of Vance-Granville Community College in Henderson, North Carolina.

support element of family literacy, together with its emphasis on child and parent relationships, makes family literacy fit easily into an overall strategy to strengthen families.

MAKE SURE THAT ADULT LITERACY EFFORTS INCLUDE FAMILY LITERACY

In some states, pressure has been building for a number of years to support adult literacy programs in general. If a family literacy initiative is under way, as it may be in response to the National Literacy Act or for other reasons, you will want to make sure that family literacy is considered an integral part of a comprehensive adult literacy policy. In Indiana, Minnesota, Mississippi, Hawaii, Illinois, and several other states, family literacy has been included as a key part of broader adult literacy strategies developed either by the governors' offices or by interagency working groups. If your state has adult literacy initiatives either in the planning stages or under active consideration by the governor or legislature, you should work to make sure that family literacy is part of the package.

DEVELOP THE EFFICIENCY ARGUMENT

One of the strongest reasons to invest in family literacy is that it has a "double bang for the buck." State policymakers, including legislators, will be influenced by the hope that they can make a single investment that will pay off in both the short term by helping the parents acquire new skills and the long term through preschool programs for the children. This argument will be partially blunted by the fact that family literacy programs are not cheap, but it will be a powerful one in the state capital when it comes time to compete for limited resources.

FINDING CHAMPIONS

To win in a political and public policy arena, you need a champion. More likely, you need many champions for family literacy. After you have built at least the rudiments of a family literacy coalition, it is time to go searching for political leaders who are willing to make a commitment of time and energy to the family literacy effort. Despite the attractiveness of the family literacy concept, this will not be easy, because political leaders are inundated with requests for support from many worthy causes.

Family literacy leaders need to present the case for family literacy to as many powerful people in the state capital as possible, including the governor, legislative leaders, and major committee chairpeople. Some will come forth as champions, if they can be convinced that family literacy programs are aimed at the right goals and that they work. Family literacy advocates now have enough evidence on both these scores to find political leaders who are willing to take risks for family literacy.

At the same time, family literacy advocates need to be aware that most political leaders are pursuing goals, such as education reform or economic development, that are somewhat broader than helping parents and children learn. This means that your ability to characterize family literacy as a program with "twice the payoff" will be crucial in finding champions at the state level.

Once the case is made and champions are secured, it will be necessary to begin putting together a family literacy initiative package that will be both substantively sound and politically feasible. If the right champions are on your side, they will provide staff help for putting together the package — including legislation if necessary and budgets — but you and your group will have to supply the initial parameters of the package.

PUTTING TOGETHER A FAMILY LITERACY PACKAGE

As an advocate of family literacy or as a state policymaker, you will have help in putting together a family literacy package that can be enacted and funded or at least proposed by the executive branch. No matter who supports family literacy, however, before the battle is over you will have to answer the same common questions that are taught to journalism students when they first learn how to write a news story. You will have to be able to tell the governor, the budget director, a legislative committee, and many others, "who, what, when, where, and how." In the policy context, these questions mean:

- Who: *Who* will be served by the initiative or program?
- What: *What* will the program do?
- When: *When* does it start and is it a permanent or "pilot" program?
- Where: *Where* will family literacy programs be provided?
- How: *How* will we implement the program, at what cost?

Let us take each of these questions and give a generic answer about family literacy that can be modified for use in your own state.

WHO?

Family literacy is a very targeted program. It aims to improve the lives of poor and dependent families with young children. These families share the following characteristics. First, they must have small children, usually between the ages of one and five. Second, one of the parents must have low literacy skills or at least not have a high school diploma. Third, almost always these families will be low income, primarily because their skill levels do not allow them to earn higher wages. Fourth, at least one parent must not be working outside the home or must be willing to take substantial time to participate after work. Finally, the parents must be motivated enough to take advantage of the program.

The implication of all these "screens" is that the number of potential participants in the program is relatively manageable. In most states, this narrows the potential participants to no more than 3 percent of families. Nationally, at least 2 million families are likely to meet these criteria. If one further narrows the criteria by excluding families already served in a program that does not allow the time for family literacy, the number drops even lower.

Even though the target population for family literacy is relatively small, the impact of the program can be large because these are the families who need the most help and whose problems cost the most if they are not alleviated. One of the major advantages of family literacy at the state level, however, is that it does not require that the governor or legislature agree to establish another large and growing entitlement program for millions of people. In a policy sense, family literacy is targeted and manageable.

WHAT?

In pursuing a family literacy initiative, it will be important to describe a coherent and workable program model. A family literacy initiative must spell out the characteristics of programs that will fulfill the state policy goals. Guidelines for programs and criteria for funding will also have to be developed. While the emphasis of the initiative may depend on what larger state goal or goals it is linked to, the family literacy initiative will have to describe a coherent model that plausibly will achieve the state's objectives.

Your family literacy initiative can be either school-based, home-based, or based in a community organization, but any state initiative should mandate at a minimum the four key elements of a family literacy program. To repeat, these are the elements:

- Provide developmental experiences for young children.
- Provide basic skills instruction to the children's parents.
- Bring parents and children together, encouraging positive interaction and support.
- Bring parents together to share experiences and overcome obstacles to family learning.

To make these concepts more concrete, you can point to successful family literacy programs, such as those found in the Kenan project, in some programs initiated through Even Start, and in other efforts such as Head Start family literacy programs. [1]

In designing the parameters for state support of community family literacy programs, statewide initiatives will address the following issues.

Eligibility. Family literacy programs should not be means tested, although they should be targeted toward poor families where possible. We recommend that statewide initiatives allow broad eligibility of parents and students. Burdening program providers with detailed means tests or other eligibility requirements based on complex funding streams is counterproductive.

Program design and curriculum. Both the early childhood and adult literacy components of family literacy programs should utilize the best practices in each of their respective fields. Pre-kindergarten programs should be developmental and include considerable parent participation. Adult literacy services should be customized to the learner and be as directly relevant to their work or family life as possible. A great deal of parent-child interaction should be built into the guidelines for a statewide program, as should the requirement for parent support.

The state has a strong responsibility to guide local providers in appropriate curricula and program criteria not only in the early childhood development part of the program, but also in the application of adult literacy instruction for the parents. States may need to focus substantial attention on the literacy services provided to parents, since these are usually less well-developed at the local level or even the state level than early childhood development techniques.

Training and professionalization. A statewide family literacy initiative should pay special attention to the need to train family literacy providers and build an infrastructure that will promote professionalism in these programs. An important part of the state role in family literacy will be to support local programs in areas such as training and professional development. The National Center for Family Literacy has begun working with states such as North Carolina, Hawaii, and others to develop training and technical assistance programs for family literacy.

If family literacy programs increase, many states will want to establish statewide institutions similar in purpose to the National Center for Family Literacy. State family literacy training and technical assistance efforts may also be appropriately provided through the state/regional literacy resources centers linked to the new National Institute for Literacy.

Funding. Advocates for statewide literacy initiatives need to make sure that funding is an integral part of any legislation or executive action. A combination of state appropriations and retargeted federal funds should be used to support family literacy programs. Or it may be possible to free up significant funds dedicated to education reform for family literacy efforts. Compared to education or welfare budgets, family literacy programs are very inexpensive. If funding is not available for statewide initiatives, pilot project or demonstration funding may be appropriate.

WHEN?

When the program will be operational and whether or not it will be a pilot or demonstration program will be key issues in any statewide debate on family literacy. The obvious answer to the "when" question is "as soon as possible." Yet careful consideration needs to be taken to build the infrastructure necessary to support local family literacy programs while launching them in communities around the state. With limited resources, it may be wise to begin to organize the support services while phasing in statewide funding of local family literacy programs.

Several states, including Hawaii and Louisiana, have taken a pilot program approach in which family literacy programs are to be tested for two years before the legislature decides to fully fund the program. This approach is reminiscent of the beginning of the Kentucky PACE program.

In the future, state legislators and administrators should have little reason to recommend pilot or demonstration funding for family literacy. Although pilot programs may be a way to get something started, family literacy advocates have enough evidence about what works in this field that they need not settle for "demonstrations" alleging to determine the effectiveness of the concept. Pilot or demonstration funding may simply be a way to keep costs down as programs are phased in. Challenge grants, such as those sponsored through a public-private collaborative effort in North Carolina, may be a good way for legislators and governors to test whether community support for family literacy is present.

WHERE?

Geographic and cultural diversity should be built into a statewide family literacy initiative. Such an initiative should provide enough funding so that programs can be started in all major geographic regions in the state, both urban and rural areas, and so that all significant cultural groups are covered as well. Maintaining geographic and cultural coverage will strengthen the attractiveness of the program and will show that family literacy can help solve problems in all communities.

Enough experience has now been logged in many different environments — from Indian reservations to big-city ghettos, to the hills of eastern Kentucky — to show that family literacy can work in a wide variety of settings. Family literacy advocates need to let political leaders know that family literacy programs can help people from their districts, no matter where they come from. Ensuring that enough resources are devoted to family literacy to serve a wide variety of people should be a key goal of a statewide initiative.

HOW?

There are two elements to this question. First, family literacy advocates must address how a statewide initiative will be implemented. What state agency will be in charge? How will it create the support structure to get new family literacy programs off the ground? Second, how much will a family literacy program cost? Where will the money come from?

The answer to the first question depends largely upon how family literacy fits into the priorities of the state government. If family literacy is seen as an integral part of education reform, it may be wise to place responsibility with the education agency. On the other hand, if family literacy has been portrayed as part of adult literacy efforts and justified as an economic development action, family literacy might better be administered by a central literacy or work-force development agency. Family literacy could be viewed as a way of fighting welfare dependency and strengthening families. In this case, it may be best administered by a human services agency. If this is the case, however, close cooperation with the education agency will be required to ensure the connection between family literacy and school and the placement of professional educators in teaching positions.

Whatever the agency, a central part of the implementation strategy will be the development of a strong, supportive infrastructure for local programs. Family literacy programs do not have a long history or strong bureaucratic ties that stretch back into the traditions of state government, as many education or job training programs do. As a result, there is no infrastructure for professional development, training, best practices, and "program folklore" to help guide newly developed program providers at the local level. The necessity for building this type of supporting structure should be recognized within the family literacy plan from the beginning. Family literacy presents an opportunity for building an infrastructure that spans state agencies and programs and brings them together in cooperative, cost-effective ways.

The second "how" question is how much will a family literacy program cost and how will funds be secured. Because the success of family literacy depends on all four program elements being delivered with high-quality staff, family literacy is not an inexpensive social program. Costs in Even Start programs have ranged from about $2,600 per family to more than $7,000 per family per year. Kenan Model programs cost about $4,000 per family per year. While these costs may seem high to some state officials, they are low in comparison to the combined benefits for both parents and children.

With state understanding of both the benefits of early childhood education and adult literacy, and given the momentum behind significant education reforms, it should be possible to argue successfully for state funding for family literacy. As state revenues rebound with the economy, state funds should be easier to pry loose for family literacy programs. Making the fiscal case, however, will require a strong show of support for family literacy as a cost-effective investment in people. The most persuasive case has been that family literacy provides a "double bang for the buck" by taking on the root causes of poverty and dependency among both children and adults.

BUILDING IN EVALUATION FROM THE START

When designing a package of state policies and programs, most advocates fail in one important respect. They fail to build into the program design a significant accountability and evaluation component. Resources often seem too limited to justify diversion of funds to accountability systems or evaluation procedures. Yet these systems are just as important as qualified instructors, safe surroundings, or a state-of-the-art curriculum.

Developing an accountability system that includes regular evaluation will distinguish statewide family literacy policy from many other proposals. Family literacy advocates believe in evaluation because they are sure that family literacy works and they want to know how to improve their programs. Obtaining resources for evaluation is often difficult, but this is why state policymakers must insist that evaluation and accountability be an integral part of any state funding of family literacy.

STATE INITIATIVES: A FEW VICTORIES SO FAR

In the section above, we have presented a somewhat idealized version of how you might go about developing a statewide family literacy initiative, and we have shown you what we think ought to be part of the package. In the short history of family literacy, policymakers in several states have been struggling with the same issues in real life. The victories and frustrations experienced in these states can teach us what to expect when we get down to work in our own states.

HAWAII

The Hawaii family literacy movement began with an interest in adult literacy. In 1987, the governor established the Governor's Council for Literacy. This Council was charged with developing programs, partnerships, and policies that would result in a literate Hawaii. This council was housed in the Governor's Office on Children and Youth. One of its first tasks was to conduct a literacy needs assessment of the state. Based on the results of this assessment, the Council began to bring together a broad array of public and private resources to address Hawaii's literacy problems. It invited the First Lady to serve as honorary chair of the Council. Workplace literacy and family literacy became the primary focuses of the Council.

A family literacy team was formed in 1989 following a statewide conference sponsored by Hawaii Pizza Hut. This team consisted of the key stakeholders in family literacy in the state—legislators and others associated with adult literacy, Head Start, early childhood education, the private sector, the university, and civic organizations. Members of this team went to Louisville, Kentucky, for training at the National Center for Family Literacy.

The families engaged in Hawaii's family literacy initiative are benefiting from the collaboration formed between the governor's office and the private sector.

Working with the National Center for Family Literacy, Governor John Waihee's office began a strategic planning process in 1989 that led to significant support for family literacy in Hawaii. Through a series of speeches in Hawaii and planning sessions on the mainland, the National Center for Family Literacy was able to help the governor's office develop plans and gain support for family literacy programs in the islands. In the spring of 1990, the Hawaiian legislature passed the Family Support Center Act, which established a two-year project "to demonstrate the effectiveness of the community-based family support center and to test different models of service delivery."[2] Under this law, two family literacy programs were also included in the demonstration.

The Governor's Office of Children and Youth decided not to stop at two demonstration programs and has developed, funded, and implemented five model projects in Hawaii. These projects serve native Hawaiians as well as many other families on the islands. The Governor's

Office of Children and Youth has also managed to stretch scarce public dollars by asking the legislature to create a special family literacy foundation that will match public funds with private contributions for family literacy. In this way, Hawaii has managed to extend the reach of public funding in tough times, preparing for better times and — it is hoped — program expansion.

The Hawaii Fund for Family Literacy was established in 1990 to assist organizations in developing and carrying out projects that support family literacy in Hawaii. The fund was initially supported by contributions from the Hawaii Community Foundation, Aloha United Way, and Hawaii's labor unions. Recognizing the importance of family literacy, First Lady Lynne Waihee and businessman John Tsui agreed to co-chair a fundraising campaign, which raised more than $1.5 million dollars. This public-private partnership is a significant investment for the future of Hawaii's families. The fund makes grants to support family literacy by funding, training, planning, and developing models, by building coalitions, and by donating small capital and supplies. Special consideration is given to projects that demonstrate strong community support through broad-based planning.

The Hawaiian experience shows how careful work within both the governor's office and the private sector can build a consensus for family literacy across an entire state. Family literacy has been included as an integral part not only of adult literacy plans but also of statewide economic development and family strengthening policies. Hawaii's use of National Center for Family Literacy and other mainland resources also emphasizes the need to build the capacity of states in performing the analytical and program design tasks that are required to develop a statewide family initiative.

NORTH CAROLINA

North Carolina's experience with family literacy began when the William R. Kenan, Jr. Charitable Trust, based in Chapel Hill, brought the innovation of family literacy to the state. The state's commitment to family literacy has been nurtured by a number of prominent North Carolinians, especially William Friday, former president of the University of North Carolina and now executive director of the Kenan Trust. Through the

*North Carolina's commit-
ment to family literacy has
been nurtured by many
prominent citizens, especially
William Friday, President
Emeritus of the University of
North Carolina and Executive
Director of the William R.
Kenan, Jr. Charitable Trust.*

Kenan project, four school districts in North Carolina received grants from the Trust and started to develop what later became the Kenan Trust Model programs.

The early success of the Kenan programs came to the attention of the Governor's Council on Literacy, which had set family literacy as a high priority. In 1991, the Council brought together policymakers, program providers, literacy volunteers, and advocates as well as many others into a symposium to discuss the future of family literacy. Action plans were drawn and many of those communities applied for the $5,000–$10,000 challenge grants to implement their plans. The challenge grant program provided seed funds to enable collaborative partners to start family literacy programs in communities all over North Carolina.

The North Carolina Community College system put up $50,000 and the Kenan Trust provided $50,000 to create a $100,000 challenge grant fund. Communities attempting to start family literacy programs often need seed money to get the process started. Sometimes, a small grant between $5,000 and $10,000 can make the difference. As a result of this effort, timed just right to coincide with Even Start and other sources of funding, North Carolina now boasts 38 family literacy programs. The Community College Board has also authorized each of its 58 campuses to offer family literacy programs.

In North Carolina, family literacy advocates worked with the educational community to support family literacy. With private foundation support, higher education institutions and community groups spearheaded the creation of a large number of programs in a short time. Although the governor's office was generally supportive, family literacy advocates did not find it necessary to pursue comprehensive state strategies or legislation to get programs authorized and under way. They chose instead to foster collaborative efforts among state and local agencies for a quick response to a common vision. By making family literacy part of the literacy mandate of powerful educational institutions, family literacy programs found an important niche in state policy.

LOUISIANA

In Louisiana, a statewide commission on literacy recommended a comprehensive literacy strategy to the governor, including a family literacy demonstration program. In April 1991, a bill to authorize family literacy demonstrations for parents and children who were within one year of entering kindergarten was introduced. Administered by the office of literacy, the demonstration program would be operated in at least 10 communities, at least one for each congressional district in Louisiana.

Although the bill was initially supported by the governor, he soon turned his attention to the difficult political race facing him at the time. The superintendent of public instruction stepped in and amended the original bill to create family literacy demonstration programs. The governor's plan to create a separate office of literacy outside the Department of Public Instruction was dropped. This legislation was passed but funding has yet to be appropriated. A new private literacy foundation has pledged to continue pressing the state government for action.

In Louisiana, the lesson of state involvement is less sanguine than elsewhere. Despite strong gubernatorial support for literacy in general and family literacy in particular, state funding was not obtained. A change in administration has thrown the future of state actions on family literacy into doubt. Nevertheless, the public support generated for family literacy has been translated into the creation of a new Louisiana Literacy Foundation, which is being supported by the private sector. To the extent that the supporters of family literacy can obtain private funding and regroup, the structure for family literacy will be in place in Louisiana.

ILLINOIS

Illinois has taken a slightly different approach to family literacy. The Illinois Literacy Resource Development Center (ILRDC) took the lead in developing and studying state policy in the area of family literacy for several reasons:

- Multiple state agencies and departments were involved in the funding and development of family literacy programs.

- These agencies and departments were represented at the local level in the development of family literacy programs.

- Family literacy programs were proliferating in Illinois and appeared to be successful in meeting the needs of the members of participating families.[3]

Family literacy initiatives at the local level in Illinois are usually a combined effort of adult education providers, prekindergarten, elementary, and middle schools, Head Start programs, and libraries. Other groups often included in a local effort are public aid, children and family services, universities, and businesses.

With support from the MacArthur Foundation, the ILRDC organized Family Literacy Policy Meetings. These consisted of five intensive days of meetings on family literacy in the summer of 1991. The meetings brought together a group of state agency personnel, service providers, legislators, and other interested parties. The purpose of these meetings was to develop a list of needs and policy recommendations for advancing family literacy

120

in the state.[4] Included in the group were representatives of the State Board of Education, the Community College Board, the Department of Public Aid, the Secretary of State's Literacy Office, and the Department of Children and Family Services.

This group recommended to the cabinet departments changes in policies that will stimulate the growth of family literacy programs throughout Illinois, where over 100 family literacy programs are now operating. This group will also help to implement the changes in agency policies that should lead to the expansion of family literacy programs statewide.

The Illinois experience shows how family literacy can benefit from the cooperation and hard work of a variety of state agencies led by a catalytic group such as the Illinois Literacy Resource Development Center. Without raising the issue much above the cabinet level, the Illinois group was able to make significant progress in supporting family literacy programs throughout the state. At the same time, they realized that many of the interagency conflicts creating obstacles to family literacy could not be resolved below the level of state cabinet officials. Targeting the right officials and stimulating them to take action were the keys to the progress made in Illinois.

Illinois family literacy advocates are still facing difficult questions of funding and of the eventual institutional home for family literacy programs. As the political and institutional environment changes, it is not clear whether it will be best to be associated with work-force-oriented literacy programs or education-oriented early childhood development programs. Illinois advocates hope to capitalize on early successes to find the right niche for family literacy within the state policy environment.

WHY WE NEED STATE LEADERSHIP

Although federal funds and community leadership have fueled the growth of family literacy in the past, state leadership in supporting family literacy will be crucial in the future. States will continue to dominate domestic policy making and will provide most of the resources for early childhood education, elementary and secondary education, and adult literacy for the foreseeable future. Among governments, states also have the most to gain from the success of family literacy programs. If family literacy spreads and is successful in reducing dependency, state costs for welfare, health care, job training, and even prisons will be reduced.

State leadership for family literacy has been somewhat slow in emerging not because state officials are not convinced of the efficacy of this approach, but because of the extremely difficult fiscal situation they faced during the first years of family literacy's emergence as a policy alternative. We can only hope that with the groundwork already laid in the states, when the fiscal environment improves, so will the ability of the states to exert leadership in support of family literacy.

ENDNOTES

[1] For more information on family literacy models, contact the National Center for Family Literacy, 401 S. 4th Avenue, Suite 610, Louisville, KY 40202 (502) 584-1133. After July 1, 1993, the Center's address will be Waterfront Plaza, 325 W. Main St., Louisville, KY 40202 (502) 584-1133.

[2] Hawaii State Legislature, "Conference Committee Report Number 81" (Honolulu: Hawaii State Legislature, April 27, 1990), 1.

[3] Illinois Literacy Resource Development Center, "Policy Report," 1991.

[4] Ibid.

Chapter 7

CHALLENGE FOR THE FAMILY LITERACY MOVEMENT

In the autumn of 1989, six national education goals were adopted by President George Bush and the nation's governors. Two of those goals — Goal 1 and Goal 5 — speak to the heart of the family literacy movement:

- **Goal 1: All children in America will start school ready to learn.**

- **Goal 5: Every adult American will be literate and will possess the knowledge and skills to compete in a global economy and exercise the rights and responsibilities of citizenship.**

Family literacy places equal emphasis on both goals. Family literacy provides both early education for children and literacy instruction for adults. Through the synergy of reciprocal learning and teaching among family members a more literate, supportive environment in the home is created.

In the spring of 1992, the National Center for Family Literacy brought together over 400 policymakers, practitioners, scholars, and political leaders to discuss how family literacy can contribute to achieving the nation's education and economic goals. Conference participants strenuously debated what needs to be done to achieve these two interdependent goals through the extension of family literacy throughout the nation.

The conference was organized to address three threads of concern within the family literacy movement: policy, practice, and research. Participants were asked to respond both formally and informally to questions whose answers might shape the course of family literacy in the future. In this chapter, we will pose the same questions addressed by the conferees about policy, practice, and research, and we will share the answers to those questions as well as additional issues raised at the conference.

People attending the conference shared a recognition that these are the first days of family literacy. The field has grown from 6 programs to over 1,000 in less than a decade. Much of the struggle for recognition and initial funding is behind us. The issues facing the field now are those of clarifying its boundaries, building a support system, setting a research agenda, and improving policy and practice.

To move on, we need a collective vision and a clear agenda. Through the vehicle of this conference, participants helped define that vision and create this agenda. Several themes that emerged from the conference are crucial to setting our future agenda.

THE NATION NEEDS A FAMILY LITERACY MOVEMENT

People involved in family literacy across the country, with the assistance and guidance of the National Center for Family Literacy, have built the foundation for a national movement. To expand and grow, several issues must be resolved.

ARRIVING AT A NATIONAL DEFINITION OF FAMILY LITERACY

In recent years, there has been growing attention to the definition of family literacy. As discussed in Chapter 1, the family literacy movement began with one program model in Kentucky. Over the years, that model has evolved, yet basic elements of the program have remained constant. At the same time, many other programs addressing one or more but not all of the goals of family literacy programs have come into being. Honest debate has ensued over how to define family literacy programs — how to recognize the value and contribution of a broad range of program types yet not lose focus of the core elements of the original family literacy model.

As a field, we must struggle with what family literacy is and what it is not; what it can promise to deliver and what it cannot; who it will serve and who it won't; and what the boundaries are between family literacy and other early childhood, adult literacy, and parenting and support programs. A pivotal agenda item for the immediate future is arriving at a definition of family literacy that provides guidance to the programs and to the public and yet does not constrain experimentation and diversity.

The definition suggested in this volume reflects the unique "family history" and lineage of family literacy programs as well as the experience of leaders in the field of intergenerational literacy programs. All four components — early childhood development, adult learning, parent and child together, and parental support — need to be present for a program to be part of the "family" of family literacy programs.

This definition takes us far, but we need to focus on further refinements as we develop family literacy programs in a variety of settings. In arriving at our definition of literacy, we need to keep in mind some guideposts identified at the conference:

- We need a functional definition of family literacy — one that focuses on what a family literacy program actually does and what the outcomes of such programs are.

- We need to fully articulate the concepts and premises of family literacy and its component parts.

- We need a broad definition of families. The movement suggests a need to view many different relationships in a family unit, and many different types of family units, as having the potential to contribute to family literacy.

- We need to clarify what we mean by literacy for families. Our expectations of literacy skill acquisition should be clarified. We need to address the issues of skill levels on the literacy continuum that are needed for the achievement of various social and economic goals. We need to question the significance of small gains in literacy skills, which may make no practical significance in terms of larger goals.

• We need a definition that provides guidance to our programs, to policymakers and the public, yet is flexible and encourages the experimentation and diversity that may be critical to the future of the movement.

CLARIFYING SERVICE DELIVERY MODELS

The field has methods of implementing the components of family literacy programs that are being disseminated through the National Center. But the Center itself as well as many of you in the field are experimenting with or considering different ways of assembling these components.

Methods currently being explored include family literacy programs based in the workplace. These models focus not only on the adult and child components but also on another goal of workplace literacy. Other methods being explored include those more geared to a broader range of family structures and models that are even more tailored to the needs and resources of their communities.

The consensus among those at the conference was that the movement should promote diversity in family literacy program models without losing sight of the basic tenets of core family literacy programs.

DEFINING THE RELATIONSHIP OF FAMILY LITERACY PROGRAMS TO OTHER SOCIAL AND EDUCATIONAL PROGRAMS

Persons participating in the conference struggled with the relationship between family literacy programs and other programs with similar or overlapping goals. They stressed the need for collaboration of family literacy providers with a broad range of education, social service, health, employment, and other programs. They perceived this collaboration to be essential to program effectiveness.

The field is replete with many ideas about how this collaboration should be effected. What is unresolved for the field is whether there are or should be *required* components of collaboration that can and should be defined as integral parts of family literacy programs, or whether the entire issue of the nature and extent of collaboration should be left to the local programs.

Collaboration with a broad range of education, social service, health, employment, and other programs seems to be essential to program effectiveness. Can we better define the nature of this collaboration? Are there other elements of collaboration that can and should be added to a model that already stresses collaboration?

STATE AND FEDERAL GOVERNMENTS NEED TO SUPPORT FAMILY LITERACY IN A COHERENT WAY

Most family literacy providers have created programs either with the help of, or in spite of, our state and federal governments. Many conference attendees were of the opinion that governmental agencies have not been very helpful in supporting the family literacy movement. With the one exception of the Even Start program, providers have had to piece support together from many different funding sources.

For state governments and the federal government to be more supportive to family literacy efforts, several issues must be addressed.

CLARIFYING FAMILY LITERACY'S PUBLIC POLICY NICHE

The states and the federal government are supporting family literacy, but their political leaders have difficulty fitting family literacy into their ways of looking at the world. Are family literacy programs "early childhood" programs with a side benefit of adult literacy, or are they "literacy" programs with a side benefit of helping our children and schools? What are they?

One way policymakers are addressing this issue is to use family literacy programs to further other state and federal goals. By linking these programs to other social and/or economic goals, they can be justified to decision makers. While this is a practical approach politically, it runs the risk of skewing the program focus and content and holding family literacy programs accountable for achieving goals for which the programs weren't designed.

To avoid these problems, the field should clarify the nature of family literacy programs in terms of their contribution to public policy and propose options for how they can be explained in the public policy arena.

127

CLARIFYING THE ROLE OF STATE AND FEDERAL GOVERNMENTS IN FAMILY LITERACY

Family literacy programs could be aided significantly if state and federal programs collaborated to fund family literacy programs. States in particular could play a coordinative role in negotiating federal and state program requirements and funding streams on behalf of family literacy providers.

A significant subset of family literacy providers are pragmatically proceeding without any expectation or concern that federal and state programs be better coordinated or aligned to local family literacy needs. These providers feel that the issues involved in providing family literacy services are essentially local in nature and that federal and state involvement only complicate an already complex coordination challenge. It should be noted that even these providers accept state and federal funds to support their programs.

Another way that governments could support family literacy programs is by identifying an institutional home for family literacy. Providers have to negotiate many different organizational units, personnel, funding streams, program regulations, and funding restrictions in order to amass sufficient funds to support their programs. If family literacy were assigned one institutional home within state government, then much of the organizational negotiations could be simplified.

FAMILY LITERACY PROGRAMS MUST BE ACCOUNTABLE

Historically, there has been great resistance in the human services field to efforts to quantify and evaluate programs. More recently, however, human service providers are realizing the importance of quantifying progress and being able to justify expenditures based on performance. Among those attending the family literacy conference, there was an unusual agreement that accountability must be a key element of the movement.

DOCUMENTING OUR SUCCESSES; LEARNING FROM OUR FAILURES

Providers of family literacy services are sure that their programs work. If our movement is to succeed, we must develop methods of documenting these results and assessing progress. To compete effectively for resources, the field will have to clarify what family literacy programs are promising to deliver and when. This brings us back to our need for a clear definition of what family literacy programs are, who they serve, how they deliver, and what they can accomplish. At the same time, we need to be sure that ten years from now we can answer difficult questions about how effective our programs are and what impact they have had on families — on children and adults, on our society and the economy.

To keep the movement on the right track, to justify expenditures, and to compete for scarce resources, the family literacy movement must develop the capacity for assessment and quality assurance. Key to developing an effective accountability system is identifying the purposes for which assessment will be used and developing different assessment techniques for each. For example, assessment must be done to measure the progress of individual adult and child participants, to measure the effectiveness of individual programs, and to make policy decisions about family literacy. Each purpose requires a different approach.

IMPROVING ASSESSMENT AND EVALUATION

In addition to clarifying the overall purposes for assessment, conference participants felt strongly that the field must broaden the types of evaluation data that are used. Numerical indicators alone were felt to be inadequate. Other measures such as case studies, evaluations by participants, community evaluations, and a broader range of types of tests were suggested as ways to form a more complete picture of progress. Using this more complete data, evaluation must be built into every family literacy program. Regional support organizations as well as the National Center for Family Literacy can contribute to a process of setting standards and measuring program outcomes.

To begin the process of accountability in the field, we must first be able to define a base line — both individual and national. Then we must decide what will constitute change and how we will measure it. We must select the indicators of change and identify short-term effects that we believe should be the causes of longer-term effects. These steps will provide us with a standard for the field and will enable us to make future judgments about the effectiveness of family literacy programs.

WE MUST BUILD AN INFRASTRUCTURE TO SUPPORT THE FAMILY LITERACY MOVEMENT

While many family literacy programs are in operation across the country, only the most rudimentary of support systems exists to help these programs improve and expand. To build upon the successes of existing programs and expand services to other families in need, we must develop the capacity to build a network of providers so that they can share their experience, provide training and technical support, and build a profession. These are the same agenda items that have been identified in the field of adult literacy for several years.

CREATING AN INSTITUTIONAL INFRASTRUCTURE

The field needs the infrastructure to translate the results of research into practice, to encourage practice-based research, to identify research needs and opportunities to the research community, to disseminate information on what works in family literacy, to build a solid network between and among programs, and to expand training.

We need to decide who will build this infrastructure and where its institutional home should be. States may be the ideal level to support this work, but states may not be ready to take the initiative. The National Center for Family Literacy has taken steps in this direction to help create an infrastructure without the assistance of government. The Center is now exploring ways to regionalize its services and link family literacy training and assistance to state resource centers. Creating this infrastructure must be a major agenda item for the future of the movement.

PROVIDING INCREASED TRAINING AND TRAINING ACROSS PROGRAMS

Related to the need for more collaboration is the need for increased training and training across programs. As with the larger field of adult literacy, program staff feel the need for more opportunities for pre- and in-service training. Because there is no real infrastructure to support family literacy programs and because program funds are limited, training opportunities are likewise limited. To be more effective and to increase our practice-based research, we need to provide more and improved training opportunities for family literacy practitioners.

In addition to more training in family literacy, conference participants stressed the need for much more training across programs. Family literacy providers eloquently describe the limitations of our categorical program approach to social problems. One provider opined, "Education professionals only want to deal with education problems; health professionals with health problems; employment professionals with job problems. Even on my own staff, my literacy professional and early childhood professional get tunnel vision. It's the professionals who must change. We must be willing to look at the person, the family, the community—focusing on our common ground rather than on our program boundaries."

To aid professionals in focusing on people, families, and communities and in working together to meet their needs, joint training could be an effective approach—at least one that conference attendees strongly felt deserves further attention.

In addition to these overall themes, the conference attendees also clarified an agenda for the field of family literacy in each of three areas: research, practice, and policy. While these agendas do not exhaust the possible themes for the family literacy movement, they do point the way and provide a framework for action. Here are summaries of the agendas developed at the first National Conference on Family Literacy.

THE RESEARCH AGENDA

The first National Conference on Family Literacy was one of the first and perhaps only times that we have brought together theoreticians and scholars from two traditions: early childhood development and adult literacy. This "meeting of the minds" produced some consensus, considerable controversy, and a long list of researchable questions.

The research community at the conference agreed that there is every likelihood that family literacy will be helpful to children and parents alike. They cautioned that family literacy programs, however, should not be viewed as a panacea to the multiple problems besetting families. Rather, it was seen as an important tool in addressing these needs.

As reflected earlier in the crosscutting theme on collaboration, improving the literacy of a family must involve a holistic approach to the family. As eloquently articulated by Heather Weiss, the ethnic community, neighborhood, or "village" must be taken into account. A narrow view of the family is too limiting given the diversity of family types that exist today. Focusing on the family in the context of the neighborhood or village opens the door to an important array of relationships that could be enormously beneficial in meeting family literacy goals.

A broad and rich research agenda awaits the movement. Issues that were seen by the researchers attending the conference as important to be addressed in the near future are as follows:

The first National Conference on Family Literacy was one of the first and perhaps only times that we have brought together theoreticians and scholars from two traditions: early childhood development and adult literacy.

DETERMINING THE OUTCOMES OF FAMILY LITERACY PROGRAMS

Researchers were concerned that we provide quantitative evidence that demonstrates conclusively the efficacy of family literacy programs. In particular, we need to know whether providing adult literacy and early childhood experiences together in the family literacy model work more effectively than when the services are provided separately.

Does family literacy break the bonds of intergenerational poverty? The field needs to be able to answer definitively the question of whether or not family literacy programs can and do break the intergenerational cycle of low literacy and poverty.

REFLECTING THE DIFFERENCES IN HISTORY AND CULTURE OF THE COMMUNITY IN WHICH FAMILY LITERACY PROGRAMS ARE OPERATING

As John Ogbu, Professor of Anthropology at the University of California at Berkeley, has pointed out, literacy programs that do not take into account or value the differences in history or culture of an ethnic community have less chance for successful outcomes. Research should be directed to identifying ways in which family literacy programs can be grounded in and place value on the culture of the persons receiving training, while at the same time upgrading the literacy skills of the participants.

EXPANDING THE CONCEPT OF THE FAMILY IN FAMILY LITERACY

How can the family literacy concept be expanded to include work with siblings, grandparents, and other surrogate parents? Shirley Brice-Heath, Professor of English, Stanford University, argues that more research needs to be done to identify the roles that persons in the family other than a parent or child might play to support family literacy. For example, how can adolescents in the family be involved in the program, either those taking on the role of substitute parents or those who need help themselves?

FITTING FAMILY LITERACY INTO A MODEL OF LIFELONG LEARNING AND WORK-FORCE EDUCATION

Tom Sticht, President of Applied Behavioral and Cognitive Science, Inc., suggests that we need an integrated model of human cognitive development throughout the life cycle. Family literacy could contribute to the development of such a model. By situating family literacy within the context of lifelong learning, family literacy providers could better define their position in the work-force education field.

The concept of family literacy can be expanded to include the participation of siblings, grandparents, and other surrogate parents.

PHOTO BY MARJORY WILKINS

SEARCHING FOR THE RELATIONSHIP BETWEEN TAUGHT AND ACQUIRED LITERACY IN FAMILY LITERACY PROGRAMS

Is literacy that is taught the same as literacy that is environmentally acquired? Virtually no research has been done on the differences, if any, between literacy skills acquired through interaction with the family, community, and educational system and those that are specifically taught when these skills have not been acquired. A related question raised by David Weikart is whether or not a literate outlook can be developed through family literacy programs.

FINDING FAMILY LITERACY'S RELATIONSHIP TO COMMUNITY CHANGE

How can communities as well as families be influenced through family literacy? This question, raised by Heather Weiss and others, raises a fundamental question of whether communities as well as families can be positively affected through family literacy programs, or whether outside changes in villages or communities will be necessary in order for family literacy programs to work.

FINDING OUT HOW PARENTS, TEACHERS, AND STUDENTS CHANGE ATTITUDES AND BEHAVIORS THROUGH FAMILY LITERACY

What do we know about the roles of parents, teachers, and students as they change through family literacy programs? Robert Popp of the National Center for Family Literacy has suggested that as families become more literate, the roles parents, children, and teachers play change. We have not documented how these roles change or what the effect of these changes is on the learning process.

In addition to addressing these specific research questions, the field of family literacy must also focus on the research process itself. One theme coming from the conference was the importance of including family literacy program participants in the research and evaluation process. Specifically, we need to determine how participants in family literacy programs can be enlisted to help in research and evaluation and how their concerns and ideas can be utilized.

Translating the results of research into policy and practice has proved to be a stumbling block to date in the field of literacy. This is primarily because there is no infrastructure to support the literacy movement. A key issue that the family literacy movement must address is how research results can be communicated clearly to program providers and be utilized effectively.

All of us can look back to the beginning of a program or a field and wish that the originators had thought more carefully about research and evaluation in the early days. These are the early days of family literacy. We are in a unique position to ask the research questions that will matter ten years from now.

Continuing research and evaluation will be important to the family literacy movement because we have raised such high expectations. Policymakers see these programs as highly efficient and useful in concept. As a result, we will have to keep a close watch on our actual results and use research to improve our practice as the movement grows and matures.

THE PRACTICE AGENDA

The field of practice of family literacy is in the forefront of the movement — well ahead of policy and research. Program practitioners are forging ahead with new forms of collaboration, new definitions of family, new types of training and assessment. Much of this activity is going on, however, without the benefit of research findings, federal or state support, or any infrastructure for training or technical assistance.

Participants at the National Conference on Family Literacy identified an agenda to improve practice in the field. These are steps that can be taken exclusive of action on the policy and research fronts. But, it is important to understand that advances in each area will complement and strengthen the others.

The "Practice" agenda ranges from learning focused on being more sensitive to the needs of the learner, to improving a network for information sharing, to using family literacy as a vehicle for reform in other areas of social policy. The agenda includes the following issues:

PROMOTING EXPERIMENTATION AND INNOVATION

How can we help providers to assume the role of researcher and evaluator in advancing the state of the art? This issue is closely related to the research agenda item, which calls on participants to become more involved in the research. Practitioners, however, can do much to advance the state of the art by assuming the roles of researcher and evaluator — by questioning current practices and observing what procedures seem to work best. The field needs experimentation to develop new approaches to family literacy and challenge our thinking in order to achieve some of the breakthroughs that will make literacy instruction more attractive to learners.

INCREASING THE SENSITIVITY OF FAMILY LITERACY PROGRAMS TO THE GOALS OF PARTICIPANTS

In order to be effective, programs must merge overall program goals with individual goals of the participants. To retain adult learners in the programs, they must see that their goals are being met. It is important at the outset to clarify the goals of the participants and to permit them to revise their goals as they proceed with the program.

ASSURING THAT PROGRAMS FOCUS ON QUALITY OUTCOMES AND THEIR RELATIONSHIP TO INDIVIDUAL GOALS

Family literacy providers attending the National Conference on Family Literacy strongly expressed their hope that programs would move beyond the simple outcomes of moving up a grade level in reading or even attaining a GED. Quality outcomes are encouraged. These include helping children with their homework in elementary and secondary school, acquiring a good job, pursuing postsecondary education, or other outcomes that will improve the quality of their lives.

Practitioners can assume the roles of researcher and evaluator by questioning current practices and observing what procedures seem to work best as they participate in the learning process.

RELATING FAMILY LITERACY TO OTHER REFORMS

The approach taken by family literacy providers of focusing on the needs of the family rather than on single problem areas could be of significant benefit in the delivery of other social and educational programs as well.

137

Through effective collaboration, other program providers can become sensitized to the importance of viewing problems in their larger context and addressing the needs of individuals and families as a whole.

DEVELOPING FAMILY LITERACY MODELS
THAT INCLUDE CROSS-CULTURAL GROUPINGS

Family literacy providers must be sure that they do not impose values that differ among cultures. To this end, the movement should develop a range of different models that respond to different family structures and build on the strengths and history of each cultural group. Where population density is not sufficient to warrant different program models, each program must be particularly sensitive to this issue, building on the diversity of its participants and the assets of each cultural group represented.

USING EXISTING NETWORKS FOR
FURTHERING GOALS OF FAMILY LITERACY

While extensive networks have not yet been established for family literacy, such networks do exist for other programs. Family literacy providers can piggyback on these networks, such as child care, employment, and family support, in order to share information among programs and take the best from these networks to build their own programs.

LINKING FAMILY LITERACY PROGRAMS
TO LIFELONG LEARNING

This agenda item is related to the concern of practitioners that programs focus on quality outcomes. For many program participants, improved literacy skills may be the first step toward expanded learning opportunities. Family literacy providers should position themselves so that there are easy connections between their literacy training and more advanced education and training opportunities. Participants should be encouraged to view their participation in family literacy programs as one part of a broad array of opportunities available to them.

THE POLICY AGENDA

The family literacy movement is being created out of the vision and dedication of hundreds of people across the country. There is not one national policy that defines family literacy; no large array of federal and state programs exists to support its cause. Its policy structure is organic, growing and changing to accommodate local conditions and needs, yet retaining the core elements that distinguish it from other program types.

Several sets of policy issues were raised at the conference. Other than the definitional issues discussed in the crosscutting themes, many of the policy issues revolve around the need for federal and state policymakers to coordinate their programs and policies to support family literacy in a collaborative way. Other policy concerns include the need to establish the relative costs of family literacy programs, to encourage more local involvement in policymaking, to promote a clearer and myth-free understanding of family literacy among the general public, and to attend to the family literacy needs of rural America.

The policy agenda emerging from the conference deliberations included the following elements.

DEFINING THE COSTS AND BENEFITS OF
FAMILY LITERACY PROGRAMS

The family literacy movement is predicated on the delivery of adult and early childhood literacy services coupled with family and group support. Common sense tells us that this arrangement must be more cost effective than providing each service independently, yet the costs have not been documented. In addition to the financial cost savings, the impact of the services is estimated to be more profound when provided in a more concentrated and focused way. These benefits have not been quantified. The public policy debate could be furthered if these costs and benefits could be better quantified.

MOVING FROM A DEFICIT MODEL OF
FAMILY LITERACY TO AN ASSETS-BASED MODEL

Many state and federal programs that can support family literacy are based on a deficit model. That is, they focus on the skills that participants *don't* have. They focus on illiteracy rather than literacy. This model is ultimately self-defeating and fails to recognize the existing skills and abilities of persons who seek to upgrade their skills. An important agenda item for the family literacy movement is to help programs move from the deficit model of family literacy to an assets-based model. The training and curriculum development activities of the National Center for Family Literacy are based on this asset or strength model. State and federal agencies must also be encouraged to adopt the more positive approach.

ENCOURAGING MORE LOCAL POLICY DEVELOPMENT AND DEBATE

Many of the problems of collaboration and coordination that face local providers could be addressed through more formalized local policymaking processes. Conference attendees recommended the formation of local think tanks, where participation would rotate among community members and the purpose would be to improve the quality and effectiveness of family literacy programs.

EDUCATING POLICYMAKERS AND THE PUBLIC ABOUT FAMILY LITERACY

A major policy task is to educate policymakers themselves about the goals of family literacy programs and the broad range of families and family types that can benefit from these programs. Similar education for the public at large is also in order. Other educational tasks include continuing to dispel the myths policymakers and the general public have about family literacy. For example, we need to stress that enhancing literacy skills takes considerable time, that almost all persons have some level of literacy skills, and that training is required in order to help persons increase their literacy skills.

While family literacy programs have grown significantly in the past decade, there are many policymakers who are still unaware of their existence and potential. The movement should focus on increasing awareness of both policymakers and the general public on the nature of family literacy programs, their potential benefits, and how they might be started.

DEFINING THE STATE ROLE IN PROVIDING SUPPORT FOR FAMILY LITERACY

Policymakers should begin to clarify what the state role is or could be in supporting family literacy programs. Specifically, what organizations are responsible for family literacy programs? How will funding be coordinated? Will training and technical assistance be provided? What will be the relationship between the states and the National Center for Family Literacy? What role will the new state literacy resource centers play?

ENHANCING THE FEDERAL ROLE IN FAMILY LITERACY

The family literacy movement would be helped by increased support as well as by clearer lines of responsibility for family literacy. Specifically, the federal government needs to decide what organization will be responsible for family literacy. Are programs other than Even Start encouraged to support family literacy programs? What role will the federal government take in public awareness, research, and improving the state of the art? Finally, as it organizes its activities, the National Institute for Literacy should make support of family literacy a key part of its agenda.

BUILDING MORE COHESION AMONG FEDERAL AND STATE POLICIES

The experience of the family literacy movement to date is that collaboration at all levels of government and delivery is necessary. Family literacy

The first National Conference on Family Literacy illustrated the power of a collective vision given voice by leaders in the field such as Sharon Darling, President of the National Center for Family Literacy. The next task is to translate this vision into reality in communities across the country.

141

providers are demonstrating the need to reorient many of our human service and educational programs to focus on families and communities. A mechanism for achieving this reorientation is needed, but the mechanism must respect the goals of other programs and at the same time not skew the goals of family literacy programs.

To pay for family literacy services, many programs have to combine support of several state and federal programs. This poses real problems for providers due to different funding cycles, eligibility guidelines, allowable costs, and program purposes. The movement could be aided by practical advice to program providers on how to effect this combined funding arrangement. States could make a major contribution to the field by assisting local providers in how to combine federal and state program funds to support family literacy programs.

The growth and development of the family literacy movement has been a bottom-up process. It has matured to the point where it is becoming a growing policy issue in the states and with the federal government. Because of the course of its development, it lacks an overall national policy framework. It is time to create this framework to solidify the movement and allow it to proceed to the next stage of development — refinement and expansion.

This first National Conference on Family Literacy was extraordinary in that it showed participants in the field the power of their collective vision. This vision is presented in the form of the agenda outlined above for the family literacy movement. Our collective task is to translate this vision into reality. To do that, we need to consider the future of the family literacy movement.

"If we can spur the

national movement,

build a family literacy

infrastructure, and

learn how to

evaluate our progress,

we will have met

our challenge

for the immediate

future."

— PARTICIPANT
FIRST NATIONAL
CONFERENCE ON
FAMILY LITERACY

Chapter 8

THE FUTURE OF FAMILY LITERACY

At the conclusion of the first National Conference on Family Literacy, leaders at the National Center for Family Literacy paused to take stock of how far the family literacy movement has come and where it might be going. In this chapter, we will approach family literacy not as a program but as a national movement. Then we will try to provide some guidance about where the family literacy movement should go next. We will try to stimulate more thinking about the future of family literacy.

THE FAMILY LITERACY MOVEMENT

National publicity on the adult literacy issue has spawned a growing movement of people committed to adult literacy. Building on years of effort by groups already active on behalf of adult education and literacy services, this movement has been able to help pass a major piece of national legislation aimed at improving literacy and basic skills across the nation.

Family literacy has developed substantial grassroots and public support, both as a subset of the larger literacy effort and as a separate thrust. Family literacy has also developed support from school reformers, who see it as a way of strengthening the readiness of children and involving parents in their children's education — two key tenets of education reform. Early childhood development advocates have discovered a new ally in the family literacy movement.

The family literacy movement has also grown as a result of hundreds of local programs starting through interest generated by the National Center for Family Literacy, the Barbara Bush Foundation, the Even Start program, and through several state and citywide initiatives. With staff drawn from disciplines such as early childhood development and adult education, these new program operators have become family literacy advocates. They are advocates not only for their own programs but also for statewide and national policies promoting family literacy. These are the first and most dedicated group of advocates in communities across the nation. Because the field of family literacy is so new, however, most of the family literacy advocates have developed professionally in one of several other fields.

As a movement, family literacy both benefits and suffers from the multiplicity of potential supporters. It benefits because otherwise disparate groups of people whose primary concerns are preschool children or low-literate adults or the reform of public schools have been able to join together in support of family literacy. Family literacy suffers, however, because many of these same people retain their loyalty in time and effort to their initial commitments in the fields of adult education, elementary and secondary education, or preschool programs.

GROWTH AT THE GRASSROOTS LEVEL

Family literacy programs have been springing up all over America. Fueled by a modest federal appropriation, significant corporate and foundation support, and an outpouring of grassroots enthusiasm, the growth of family literacy has been extraordinary. The figure on page 145 presents a conservatively estimated picture of the growth of programs.

The growth rate in family literacy programs has been rapid and has more than doubled to over 1,000 programs reported by the National Center for Family Literacy in 1993. The total number of families now

THE GROWTH OF FAMILY LITERACY

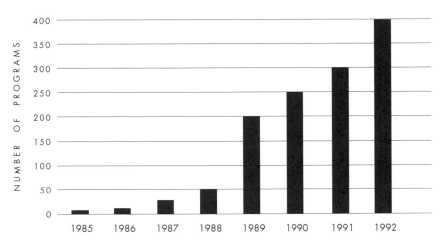

Note: By the end of 1993, it is projected there will be 1,000 family literacy programs.
Source: National Center for Family Literacy

served across the nation is still less than about 30,000. Since we estimate the demand for family literacy may be as high as a million families, there is plenty of room for growth. Judging from the response to the grant programs of the Toyota Motor Company, the rate of increase of the Even Start program, and the intensity of activity in the states — even during a severe recession — the prospects for growth in family literacy programs and coverage are bright. At the same time, as more people outside program operations themselves learn about family literacy, a greater diversity of family literacy supporters is likely to emerge at the grassroots level, in the state capitals, and in Washington.

At the grassroots level, the family literacy movement is thriving. The outpouring of interest in the first National Conference on Family Literacy attests to the constituency for family literacy across the nation. Although the conference could only accommodate 425 participants, at least three times that many asked for invitations. Participants came from all 50 states and represented virtually every aspect of America's population.

As we reported in Chapter 6, the deliberations of the conference showed very clearly that there is a need for a family literacy movement, and that the movement grows each day at the grassroots level. We also pointed out that the grassroots movement is ahead of the national leadership's ability to service the movement's needs in research, policy, and practice.

While the movement spreads and grows stronger at the local level, the family literacy movement at the state and national levels is considerably weaker. Less strength at the national and state levels is not a disadvantage in the short run because it reflects that the movement has not generated from the top down. In the long run, however, the combination of too few resources at the state and regional level and the national leadership being stretched too thin may serve to blunt the growth of family literacy as a movement and as a policy approach. Many of the issues raised at the conference dealt with these questions about the family literacy movement and its future.

We would like to suggest a few answers to the questions raised at the conference by daring to prescribe what each of us might do to strengthen the family literacy movement. We presume to provide general guidance on three key questions:

- Where should we go from here?
- How can we build an infrastructure to support family literacy?
- What can each of us do to help?

WHERE SHOULD WE GO FROM HERE?

As a policy idea and as a movement, family literacy is on the verge of blossoming into a major national force. Family literacy deals with the root causes of poverty and intergenerational dependency through education. Family literacy is attractive to leaders in education, business, and government because it addresses these problems by supporting the family. Family literacy is also timely because it addresses several national education goals at once in a cost-effective way. Finally, family literacy has support because it delivers what it promises.

At the grassroots level, family literacy has taken root and is spreading as fast as resources will allow. At the state and national level, significant recognition has been built that will allow family literacy to prosper during the next few years. All that is missing is a commitment from the family literacy movement to set ambitious national goals and pursue them.

At the first national conference on family literacy, we saw and felt a stirring among supporters of family literacy of a new confidence in their ideas, programs, and solutions for national problems. We believe that family literacy advocates need not—should not—stay at home and focus entirely on problems in their own communities. Although family literacy begins at home, it needs a national vision to survive and flourish.

The future of family literacy requires that we set our own goals. We submit three goals for discussion and debate both within and outside the family literacy movement:

- **Goal 1: To provide family literacy opportunities for at least one million families across America by the year 2000.**

- **Goal 2: To build an infrastructure that will support family literacy programs in every community in America.**

- **Goal 3: To improve, assess, evaluate, and improve again the effectiveness of every family literacy program in America.**

PROVIDING FAMILY LITERACY NATIONWIDE

Millions of poor families will pass through the stage of life where family literacy can help them the most during the period from now until the year 2000. Family literacy programs are now serving fewer than 30,000 families per year, implying that at the current rate we will be able to reach only about 200,000 families by the turn of the century. We will need to expand our efforts about tenfold in a little less than a decade to meet this goal.

Because we have good models of family literacy programs that can be replicated successfully, it is reasonable to assume that the application of more resources would result in high-quality programs being developed in communities across the nation. Much of the developmental work on model family literacy programs has been done. Now we can go into full production if we have the will, the ways, and the means.

The total price tag for serving a million families over the decade will be less than $5 billion, a small fraction of the annual national spending on any one of the other functions such as education, welfare, health care, or defense. The family literacy movement should strongly advocate that the federal and state governments and the private sector share the task of allocating at least this level of resources to family literacy over the remainder of the decade. We have strong evidence that family literacy is a good investment. We should challenge the economic and political leaders of our country to make that investment now.

BUILDING A NATIONAL INFRASTRUCTURE

More resources are necessary to meet current needs, but money alone will not be enough. We also need to build the network of services required to expand our efforts tenfold in a decade. To make sure that family literacy programs are delivered skillfully and are of the highest quality, we need to build a national infrastructure of training and assistance services that can help communities implement family literacy programs successfully.

Since family literacy deals with small children and adults who may be taking their last opportunity to learn new skills, we have a special responsibility to offer high-quality programs that really work for the people we are trying to serve. This means that communities that start and operate family literacy programs need high-quality help, the type of help that is provided now by the National Center for Family Literacy.

Family literacy can provide new hope for thousands of children and their parents in communities across the nation.

As the family literacy movement grows, it will also require an expanded support structure so that innovations, best practices, and research and evaluation can be shared. Policy development in the states will also mean that a great deal of information will need to be gathered and communicated to the field. As the field of family literacy takes shape, there will be a growing need to service the needs of family literacy professionals.

If the family literacy movement is to grow and serve many more people, these needs will have to be met. These needs cannot be met through the current capacity of organizations such as the National Center for Family Literacy or other groups at the national level. It seems clear that the capacity of the National Center will have to be enhanced and that some sort of state or regional support structure will have to be organized. In addition, the new National Institute for Literacy should probably play a role in helping to build an infrastructure to support family literacy's growth and development.

The shape and structure of a national infrastructure for family literacy will have to be determined by the hard work of many in the movement over the next few years. That we need to start building one is not at issue, however. We need to get started right away, and this implies that everyone interested in family literacy needs to pay at least some attention to events outside their own communities, in their state capitals, and in the nation as a whole.

CONTINUOUS QUALITY IMPROVEMENT IN FAMILY LITERACY

The family literacy movement has been fortunate that its leadership has recognized from the start the responsibility to promote continuous quality improvement in the field. Family literacy researchers, policymakers, and —most of all—practitioners realize that in an imperfect world no program is ever perfect. Although we think we have a workable approach to family literacy, we know that continuous assessment, evaluation, and improvement is the only way to meet our responsibilities to children, parents, funding organizations, the public, and — ultimately — ourselves.

This means that groups such as the National Institute for Literacy, the National Center for Family Literacy, state and regional organizations, and local community groups must recommit themselves to a cycle of continuous improvement in family literacy. We must be accountable and willing to listen to the results of research and evaluation. We must also build new structures to finance, carry out, and communicate evaluative research in the field of family literacy.

These three goals are ambitious but not impossible to achieve. With hard work and a few breaks, family literacy can provide new hope for thousands of children and their parents in communities across the nation. By focusing our attention on three immediate goals, we can ensure the future of family literacy.

WHAT EACH OF US CAN DO TO HELP

This book has been written for several audiences. It is intended to educate people about what family literacy is, where it came from, and how they might become involved in an exciting and growing movement. It is also intended to air many of the questions posed by those already in the movement about the future of family literacy. For those who have been convinced that family literacy is worth working on, or that family literacy requires renewed commitment, we offer a list of things each of us can do to help spread family literacy across the nation.

- *Community leaders* can identify needs and benefits of family literacy and work to create programs in your areas.
- *Business leaders* can take the initiative to develop workplace literacy programs for adults and combine their efforts with family literacy programs.
- *School leaders* can initiate family literacy programs to better prepare children for school and increase the involvement of parents in the education of their children.
- *Urban officials* can begin public/private family literacy initiatives to develop a comprehensive approach to urban problems such as poverty, unemployment, and the need for community development in public housing.
- *State officials* can recognize the importance of family literacy plays in fulfilling other state goals and coordinate and target state and federal programs to support family literacy.

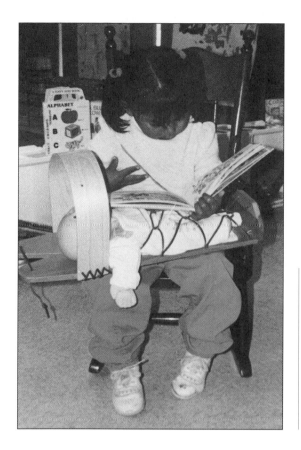

Family literacy improves the lives of our children today and creates a promising future for all the generations that follow.

- *National officials* can take the lead in promoting public awareness about family literacy, supporting research on family literacy, and developing and sharing best practices.
- *Literacy and early childhood education advocates* can combine their services to further the goals of family literacy.
- *Members of the public* can become better educated about the benefits of family literacy and serve as advocates for the creation of programs to serve their communities.

The family literacy movement has just begun. There is room and a need for many different hands to help shape the future of family literacy. We *can* help improve the lives of our children. We *can* help strengthen our families and improve our schools. We *can* help to better prepare our work

151

force. These are goals well within our reach. To do this, we need creativity. We need dedication. We need people who will reach across the boundaries of programs and agencies to realize our shared vision. We invite you to become a part of this movement to make our shared vision a reality.

BIBLIOGRAPHY

Abt Associates, Inc. & RMC Research Corporation. *National Evaluation of the Even Start Family Literacy Program.* Washington, DC: U.S. Department of Education, October 28, 1991.

American Association for Adult and Continuing Education. *The Capitol Letter.* Washington, DC: AAACE, August 30, 1991.

Barbara Bush Foundation for Family Literacy. *First Teachers.* Washington, DC: The Barbara Bush Foundation for Family Literacy, 1989.

Barrios, Joseph. "Family Pact: Sunnyside Program Educates Both Parents and Children." *Tucson Citizen,* November 23, 1991.

Berrueta-Clement, John R., et al. *Changed Lives: The Effects of the Perry Preschool Program on Youths Through Age 19.* Ypsilanti, MI: High/Scope Educational Research Foundation, 1984.

Brizius, Jack, & Susan Foster. *Enhancing Adult Literacy: A Policy Guide.* Washington, DC: Council of State Policy and Planning Agencies, 1987.

Business Council for Effective Literacy. "Adult Literacy: Programs, Planning, Issues." New York: Business Council for Effective Literacy, No. 31, April 1992.

Charlotte Observer Review. "On A Cold Day in August, Literacy Fund to Benefit from Business Equipment Sales." *The Charlotte Observer,* August 5, 1991.

Chisman, Forrest, & Associates. *Leadership For Literacy : The Agenda for the 1990s.* San Francisco, Oxford: Jossey-Bass Publishers, 1990.

Commonwealth of Kentucky. "HB 300: An act relating to support services for families." Lexington, KY: 1988.

Commonwealth of Kentucky. "House Bill No. 544." Lexington, KY: January 29, 1988.

Dallas County Adult Literacy Council. *Literacy Update.* Dallas, TX: Dallas County Adult Literacy Council, Fall 1991.

Darling, Sharon. "Breaking the Cycle of Educational Failure: The Family Literacy Model." Southern Education Foundation's Continuing Conference, November 8, 1990.

Darling, Sharon. *The Challenge of Eliminating Illiteracy.* Louisville, KY: National Center for Family Literacy, May 18, 1989.

Darling, Sharon. "Family Literacy: A simple idea that's making at-risk parents and children collaborators in success." Southern Education Foundation's Continuing Conference, November 8, 1990.

Darling, Sharon. *Family Literacy: The Need and the Promise.* Louisville, KY: National Center for Family Literacy, February 19, 1992.

Darling, Sharon. *Family Literacy and the Nation's Goals for Education.* Louisville, KY: National Center for Family Literacy, 1991.

Darling, Sharon, Robert Popp, & Don Seaman. *Follow-up Study of the Impact of the Kenan Trust Model for Family Literacy.* Louisville, KY: National Center for Family Literacy, Spring 1991.

Education Week. "Philanthropy." *Education Week*, Vol. XI, No. 22, February 19, 1992.

Hayes, Andrew E. "Undoing the Oversimplification of a Complex Matter: Issues in Defining Evaluative Criteria, Data Collection, and Reporting for Intergenerational Literacy Programs." Wilmington, NC: The University of North Carolina at Wilmington and The National Center for Family Literacy, AERA Symposium, 1991.

Hearn, Patti, S. "Bridging the Skills Gap Business and Professional Women." *River City News & Views*, May 1991.

HIPPY, USA. "HIPPY: Home Instruction Program for Preschool Youngsters." New York: HIPPY, USA, 1991.

Illinois Literacy Resource Development Center. *The Mechanics of Success for Families: An Illinois Family Literacy Report , Family Literacy Programs, Report #1.* Rantoul, IL: Illinois Literacy Resource Development Center, 1990.

Illinois Literacy Resource Development Center. *Illinois Policy Report.* Rantoul, IL: Illinois Literacy Resource Development Center, 1991.

Kamuf, Rachael. "Waging War: Louisville-based Center Fights Illiteracy Battle." *Business First*, Vol. 8, No. 27, February 3, 1992.

Kanfer, Stefan. "Good Things, Small Packages." *Time*, July 29, 1991.

Kirkpatrick, Diane W. "Family Literacy: Doorway to Hope." *Horizons*, May/June, 1991.

Lawson, Matt. "Parents and Children Learn Together." *Mississippi Press Plus*, December 4, 1991.

Lucke, Jamie. "Parent-Child Program is National Education Model." *Lexington Herald-Leader*, January 15, 1991.

Marriot, Michel. "When Parents and Children Go to School Together." *The New York Times*, August 21, 1991.

Mississippi Governor's Office for Literacy & the Mississippi Literacy Foundation. *State Literacy Strategies: A Policy Primer.* Jackson, MS: Mississippi Literacy Foundation, 1989.

National Center for Adult Literacy. "Abstracts of R & D Projects — 1992." Philadelphia: University of Pennsylvania, January, 1992.

National Center for Family Literacy. "Family Literacy Program Shows Promise in Raising Literacy Levels in America's 'At-Risk' Families." Louisville, KY: National Center for Family Literacy, August 1991.

National Center for Family Literacy. "Follow-Up Studies: The Children." Louisville, KY: National Center for Family Literacy, January 1991.

National Center for Family Literacy. "A Guide to Funding Sources for Family Literacy." Louisville, KY: National Center for Family Literacy, November 11, 1991.

National Center for Family Literacy. "Model Sites Follow-up Study." Louisville, KY: National Center for Family Literacy, June 1991.

National Center for Family Literacy. "National Center for Family Literacy Newsletter." Louisville, KY: National Center for Family Literacy, Winter 1991.

National Center for Family Literacy. "National Center for Family Literacy Newsletter." Louisville, KY: National Center for Family Literacy, March 1992, Vol. 4, Issue 1.

National Center for Family Literacy. "News From the National Center for Family Literacy." Louisville, KY: National Center for Family Literacy, Fall/Winter 1989, Fall 1990.

National Center for Family Literacy. *Spreading the Word, Planting the Seed.* Louisville, KY: National Center for Family Literacy Newsletter, 1991.

National Center for Family Literacy. *Toyota Families for Learning Quarterly Report: August 26, 1991.* Louisville, KY: National Center for Family Literacy, August 26, 1991.

National Center for Family Literacy. "What Parents Say About Participation in Family Literacy Programs." Louisville, KY: National Center for Family Literacy Newsletter, June 25, 1991.

National Center for Family Literacy and Project Literacy, U.S. "A Special Report on Family Literacy." Pittsburgh, PA: WQED/PLUS, Spring 1990.

National Clearinghouse on Literacy Education. "CAL NCLE Notes." Washington, DC: Center for Applied Linguistics, Vol. 1, No. 2, December 1991.

National Governors' Association. *New Frontiers for Lifelong Learning.* Washington, DC: National Governors' Association, 1991.

National Governors' Association State Literacy Exchange & Mississippi Employment Security Commission, Mississippi Governor's Office for Literacy. *Assessing the Nation's Literacy: A State Policy Primer.* Washington, DC: National Governors' Association, 1991.

Nickse, Ruth S. "A Typology of Family and Intergenerational Literacy Programs: Implications for Evaluation." Brookline, MA: Nickse Associates, April 3, 1991.

Parents in Education. "Series of Ten Even Start Family Literacy Focus Papers." Portsmouth, NH: RMC Research Corporation.

Popp, Robert J. *Past and Present Educational Experiences of Parents Who Enrolled in Kenan Trust Family Literacy Programs.* Louisville, KY: National Center for Family, November 20, 1991.

Popp, Robert J. *Summary of Research for the Kenan Trust Model Family Literacy Programs.* Louisville, KY: National Center for Family Literacy, July 3, 1991.

Putka, Gary. "Teaching Aides: Schools Now Give Parents Crucial Roles in Educating Children." *The Wall Street Journal*, December 30, 1991.

Reading Is Fundamental. *A Guide to RIF's Family Literacy Programs.* Washington, DC: Reading Is Fundamental, 1991.

RMC Research Corporation. "Ask About Chapter 1: Questions Parents Often Ask About Chapter 1 Programs." Hampton, NH: Chapter 1 Parent Involvement Center, RMC Research Corporation, Fall 1990.

RMC Research Corporation. "How Families Teach, Support, Learn, Make Decisions." Hampton, NH: Chapter 1 Parent Involvement Center, RMC Research Corporation, Fall 1990.

Rolf, Carol. "Family Learning Center Explained." *West Memphis Evening Times*, March 26, 1991.

Santopietro, Kathleen, and Joy Kreeft Peyton. "Assessing the Literacy Needs of Adult Learners of ESL." *ERIC Digest*, October 1991.

Skelly, Mary, E. "Living Illiterate... Programs at Work." *School and College*, June 1991.

Southport Institute for Policy Analysis. "Small Businesses Face Skills Crisis." Washington, DC: Southport Institute for Policy Analysis Press Release, May 19, 1992.

St. Pierre, Robert G., et al. "National Evaluation of the Even Start Family Literacy Program — Status of Even Start Projects During the 1990–91 Program Year: Second Year Report." Cambridge, MA: Abt Associates, Inc., and Portland, OR: RMC Research Corporation, April 1992.

State of Hawaii House of Representatives, Fifteenth Legislature. "H.B. Number 2281, H.D. 2, S.D. 2: A Bill for an Act Relating to Family Support Centers." Honolulu, HI: State of Hawaii House of Representatives, 1990.

State of Illinois. "Ayude a su hijo a leer y aprender." Springfield, IL: State Literacy Office, May 1991.

State of Louisiana House of Representatives, Regular Session 1991. "R.S. 17:3933: Establishes a Family Literacy Demonstration Program in the Office of Literacy." Baton Rouge, LA: State of Louisiana House of Representatives, 1991.

Steinberg, Carol. "In Three Districts, Parents Learn to Read to Help Their Children." *The New York Times*, January 27, 1991.

Sticht, Thomas. "Getting WELL: Workforce Education and Lifelong Learning." San Diego: Applied Behavioral and Cognitive Science, Inc., 1992.

Student Coalition for Action in Literacy Education. *Foresight!* Chapel Hill, NC: UNC–Chapel Hill, Vol. 2, No. 1, January/February 1992.

Texas A & M University System. "Illiteracy Threatens America Says Sharon Darling." *Quatrefoil*, Summer 1991.

Tousignant, Marylou. "A Chance at Starting Even." *The Washington Post*, January 22, 1992.

United States Department of Education. *Even Start: Abstracts 1989*. Washington, DC: Government Printing Office, 1991.

United States Department of Education. *Even Start Family Literacy Programs Statute*. Washington, DC: United States Department of Education.

United States Department of Education. *Chapter 1 Flexibility: A Guide to Opportunities in Local Projects*. Washington, DC: Office of Elementary and Secondary Education, February 1992.

United States Department of Health and Human Services. *Promoting Family Literacy Through Head Start*. Washington, DC: United States Department of Health and Human Services, DHHS Publication No. (ACF) 91-31266, 1991.

United States Department of Housing and Urban Development. "Educational Achievement Lags in Public Housing." Washington, DC: United States Department of Housing and Urban Development, HUD 92-24, April 13, 1992.

United States Department of Housing and Urban Development. *Literacy and Education Needs in Public and Indian Housing Developments Throughout the Nation*. Washington, DC: United States Department of Housing and Urban Development, February 1992.

United States Government. "Federal Register: Department of Education, Even Start Program; Final Regulations and Notice Inviting Applications." Federal Register, Vol. 54, No. 55, March 23, 1989.

Weinstein-Shr, Gail. "Family and Intergenerational Literacy in Multilingual Families." *ERIC Q&A*, August 1990.

Wiley, Terrence. "Measuring the Nation's Literacy: Important Considerations." *ERIC Digest*, July 1991.